ARE THERE
HORSES
IN
HEAVEN?
AND OTHER THOUGHTS

Are There Horses in Heaven?

ARE THERE HORSES IN HEAVEN?
and Other Thoughts

Sermons Preached In The Shadyside Presbyterian Church
Pittsburgh, Pennsylvania

by

F. Morgan Roberts,
Pastor 1985 - 1994
Pastor Emeritus 1994

ARE THERE HORSES IN HEAVEN?
And Other Thoughts

By F. Morgan Roberts

Published by:

 Lighthouse Point Press
Riverside Commons
700 River Avenue, Suite 216
Pittsburgh, PA 15212

Copyright © 1996 by F. Morgan Roberts
Printed in the United States Of America
Library of Congress Catalog Card Number 95-082040

Publisher's Cataloging in Publication Data
Roberts, F. Morgan, 1928-
Are There Horses in Heaven?: And Other Thoughts/by F. Morgan Roberts
        p.   cm.
1. Inspirational
2. Religious
ISBN 0-9637966-4-X: $20 Hardcover

Book Design and Cover Illustration by John McCue Design Consultants
This book is printed on acid-free stock.

Second Printing, August 1996

Foreword

One of Morgan Roberts' great gifts is his ability to help us recognize the little one (the disenfranchised, the weak, the scared, the disabled) in each one of us. Hearing (reading) his preaching, we come to know that we are all in need of God's love; and what's more, we all have it.

Thanks be to you, Morgan, for preaching the good news -- the best news of all times -- and doing it with such powerful grace. Thanks for collecting really good sticks and sharing them with those of us who feel your encouragement to keep on building.

Fred Rogers
Mister Rogers' Neighborhood
Pittsburgh, Pennsylvania

Are There Horses in Heaven?

C O N T E N T S

Sermons from the Shadyside Pulpit

Introduction

I would much rather be heard than read. My reason for saying that is to disclaim all credit (or else, escape blame) for the idea of publishing this book. I have never wanted to be remembered by written sermon manuscripts, mostly because I have never carried them into the pulpit with me. While I have always prepared a full manuscript, the live sermon has always been something other than the written one. Nearly always, some material is omitted because, in the process of delivery, it just doesn't fit. At the same time, other new material is added because, in reviewing the manuscript on Saturday, new thoughts are scribbled into the margins. Such illegible inspirations continue to be scrawled upon the pages right up to the moment of delivery. While it may seem a disorderly approach to the "sacred desk," it is the manner in which I have spoken from the heart across my 42 years of preaching. Because of that, the best way to appreciate the sermons in this book is to find someone who might lend you one of the many sermon tapes which may still be around. You'll have to beg or borrow, because it was my request that Shadyside Church would no longer reproduce and circulate my sermon tapes following my retirement. My voice had been heard long enough, and it was now time for a new pastor and a new voice. For those who might conceivably want to study the tapes, they now repose in the Pittsburgh Theological Seminary Library.

So what you have here are the written manuscripts from which the sermons began their weekly journey toward the live event in the pulpit. Something of the flavor of the moment of happening will be missing -- something that was supplied by those of you who shared these sermons with me. Don't ever forget: those who listen patiently and lovingly to sermons, week after week, are helping to form the very sermons that they are hearing. The love and patience of a worshipping congregation are a large (maybe the largest) element in the creation of sermons. Sermons don't happen in a vacuum; indeed, without the people in the pew, real sermons don't happen at all. Whatever remains on manuscript paper is not the real thing; the real thing begins happening during the moment of delivery. Indeed, the moment of preaching is only the beginning of the sermon. The lasting existence of a sermon is not in a book, but in the hearts and lives of people. If a sermon fails to become a vehicle of change in the lives of people, no book can preserve it!

Something else will be missing in the pages that follow. I refer to the extensive introductory comments upon the scripture lessons which preceded each sermon. During my latter years at Shadyside, these study and discussion guides were printed and distributed weekly, so that, in the moments before the service, and also during the following week, worshippers could reflect upon both scripture and sermon. Except for a few, most have been omitted from this book because of their previous publication, as well as for the purpose of making room for more sermons.

Another problem about parts of these sermon manuscripts, at least for some readers, will be the seemingly glaring neglect of inclusive language, especially in the earliest sermons. While this defect could have been corrected, I have let each manuscript stand as it was at the time. As such, it will constitute an honest admission that I was not, at that time, into inclusive language. Sometimes, in the moment of delivery, I did make verbal corrections of an inclusive nature. If this is a disturbing defect, I apologize; however, my present views on women in the church are fairly well stated in such sermons as "Beginning All Over Again," and also in "A Church Full Of Winners." I hope that these sermons will gain me some forgiveness for instances of language that are not inclusive. It is a language that I want to speak more fluently.

Any profits derived from the sale of this volume will go to the library of the Louisville Presbyterian Theological Seminary. Some of the happiest moments of my life and ministry, times of reflection and discovery, were spent in the stacks and nooks of that library during the years of my Louisville pastorate.

I will not attempt to list all of those who should be thanked for helping with this book. The list would reach back into the past, backward into the early years of ministry when it would never have occurred to me that a book of my sermons would ever be printed. While I offer special thanks to the faithful staff and beloved members of Shadyside Church, my gratitude goes to all of those who, over many years, with love, patience, encouragement and forgiveness, have helped me "find the words" with which to speak some good word for the Lord Jesus. To find, week after week, just one simple word that glorifies Christ is, after all, what preaching is about.

Morgan Roberts

$\mathcal{A}$re There Horses in Heaven?

....

September 21, 1986

Scripture Lesson: ***Revelation 19: 11-16.***

COMMENTS ON THE LESSON

$\mathcal{M}$ost biblical references to the horse are in connection with war. In somewhat the same way as some Christians were suspicious of the newfangled automobile and wanted to stay with the old-fashioned reliability of the horse (a distrust that is perpetuated still today by the Amish who believe that the automobile contributes to the disintegration of family and community life -- a distrust similar to that which some of us may have had about television when it first invaded our homes, similar also to the distrust that some of us may have about computers), early Hebrews were suspicious and slow to accept the horse. The horse was a symbol of pagan luxury and aggressiveness, and also of dependence upon human power in war. Psalmists and prophets thus warn against trusting in horses rather than the Lord. In contrast to this, the messianic king of peace in Zechariah comes riding on an ass (Zechariah 9: 9-10).

It appears that Solomon brought the horse into the mainstream of Hebrew life. Considering his many other unwise decisions, it may have been one of his few wiser moves. At some point, it became acceptable to use the horse in a poetic sense as a heavenly creature. Elijah is carried up to heaven by a chariot and horses of fire. Heavenly horses appear in the prophecies of Zechariah. In similar fashion, supernatural horses appear in the apocryphal book of 2 Maccabees and in the New Testament book of Revelation. It is from one of these texts in Revelation that we are reading.

SERMON

The initial thoughts for this sermon came flooding in upon me during an early morning walk in August. In the mail I had received a request for a contribution to support a campaign to halt the brutal killing of more than two million kangaroos a year in Australia. In a somewhat different vein, I heard from a friend about a neighbor of hers who was grieving over the death of her little dog. Her neighbor was wondering about that childlike question which, for some of us, will never go away: "Will my little dog be in heaven?"

Compared to the greater issues of the day, such as world hunger and the battle against AIDS or apartheid, as well as to other issues over which Christians debate, it did not seem to me that the issues of kangaroo welfare or canine immortality were worth sermon breath. Before I returned from my morning walk that day, I had discovered some prior questions that needed to be asked. Upon first thought, it may not seem very important to ask whether horses, dogs, and kangaroos will have an eternal life. Asking the question, however, led me to some simpler, prior questions that are of biblical and spiritual importance. Let me share them with you.

I - WILL JESUS BE IN YOUR HEAVEN?

What a stupid question? Of course, we say, Jesus will certainly be in heaven. Heaven is what Jesus is about. Jesus is what heaven is about. Jesus is how you get into heaven. Jesus is the way, the truth, and the life by which we enter the heavenly Father's presence. Jesus is what makes heaven heaven. At least, those are the customary orthodox answers to the question, "Will Jesus be in heaven?"

I was not, however, thinking about the orthodox views and answers about a heaven. Instead, I was thinking in the most common terms about what most of us mean about heaven. There is a sense in which heaven becomes a future projection of our present agenda, a sense in which many Christians believe in heaven in the same manner in which all people hope for "something pleasant" in the hereafter.

Several months ago, when someone meeting me for lunch was late in arriving, I spent a valuable half hour overhearing the conversation at the next table at which six businessmen were seated. At first, they were engaged in a vigorous discussion of business problems. At some point, the problems were resolved, and they turned to discuss their various weekend plans. From weekend plans, the discussion moved on to summer vacation plans. When these had been shared, the subject became that of retirement hopes and plans. I noted that the common thread in their conversation was the hope for some kind of desirable hereafter.

All of us are always looking forward to something, hoping for a better future. At the end of every working day, we look forward to some kind of relaxation. At the end of every week, we look forward to some kind of weekend rest. At the end of many weeks, we look forward to some kind of vacation. At the end of many years, we look forward to the big vacation, retirement. At the end of life, then what? The last big weekend? The real vacation? The ultimate retirement? What do we really mean by heaven? Is it anything more than the perfected projection of all our future agendas? Is it anything more than the reunion of our crowd, with complete isolation from all of those who make our life a hassle?

Do we envision a Palm Desert resort, or will there be, as at our cabin, a quiet lake without water-skiers? Do we see miles of virgin forests, teeming with wildlife, in which the booming guns of hunters will not be heard. What do we see in our vision of heaven?

Let me say this gently, but seriously. I'm not so sure we always see Jesus in our heaven. Yes, Jesus is there at the gate to greet us, just as Sally (Mrs. Roberts), when she managed a hotel, would often be in the lobby to meet special guests. Jesus is there, as owner of the resort, passing from table to table, chatting with the guests about the meal and the accommodations, but then passing on, leaving us to our conviviality with our old friends. Notice how, so very often, Jesus is no more than the guarantor of our continuing personal agendas. Heaven is where we will take up where we left off with our old crowd. At funerals, we greet our bereaved friends, offering them the assurance that the old bridge or poker game is certainly being resumed. The party will go on, and Jesus will smile upon us benevolently as we enjoy ourselves forever.

Surely, you must admit that such a vision lacks the spiritual quality and moral vitality of New Testament truth. In the scriptural visions of Revelation, the gathered multitude is somehow larger than our crowd. The garment of the heavenly Jesus is not the dinner jacket worn by the captain of the Love Boat. The king's robe has not been dry cleaned. Instead, it is the same old robe and still stained with blood! The wounds in his hands and side have not been dressed. He rides upon a war horse, and those who ride with him, still carry the marks of their battles. Somehow we know that they have endured hunger, privation, imprisonment, and persecution in the king's battles. There has been a battle in which the king has fought for their liberation. The joy of heaven is not like the frivolous fun of a Florida resort. The joy of heaven is the final victory of the king's love and justice over the powers of darkness. No, very definitely, this is not our usual crowd!

Is that bloody Jesus in your heaven? Does that bloodstained battalion look like your familiar circle of friends? Is the King's battle your battle in this present world? The business of the church and of the Christian is to be engaged in a battle to establish the kingdom: the rule of God's love and justice in this world. Let us never think that the battle to establish Christ's kingdom in this world of selfishness, racism, and injustice will be something as polite as a golf game. It will require some hunger and sweat. It may even require some blood. When that battle is over, heaven will be the victory banquet of those who have been a part of that battle for the kingdom of our God and of his Christ.

You see why I say that before we can talk about the possible immortality of your dog or cat, and even before we can get to the matter of eternal rest and reunion with your favorite people, we must ask if the Jesus of the New Testament is in your heaven. After all, that bloody Jesus and the kingdom of love and justice for which he died is what heaven is about. Is Jesus in your heaven?

II - ARE YOUR ENEMIES IN YOUR HEAVEN?

I suspect that our answer to this question may have more to do with our eternal destiny than we can begin to imagine. I ask that question because, as strange as it may seem, there are people who call themselves Christians for whom heaven would not really be heaven unless their enemies were in some kind of a hell. For some people, heaven wouldn't be heaven without a hell for certain others. For some so-called Christians, the joy of heaven is like that of a very exclusive inner circle which exists for the purpose of providing the delight of keeping others outside of the circle. In Revelation, it says of the heavenly city that "its gates shall never be shut by day -- and there shall be no night there." But for some Christians, a heaven without a closed door to keep their enemies out wouldn't be a real heaven at all. Even for some "born again" Christians, there are certain people who are unforgivable, people who just don't belong in their heaven.

Let's talk about those kangaroos. The brochure that came in the mail said that, for the year 1986, the Australian government has set a quota that will allow the hunting and killing of 2,683,700 kangaroos. In western nations, there is a market for their hides and also for their meat as pet food. These quiet vegetarian animals are shot or bludgeoned to death, and the numbers being killed could threaten their extinction. At least, that's what the brochure said. I'm sure that the Australian government has some answer to these charges, and I would be delighted to receive any information that government could furnish. I always like to hear both sides of a story.

I mention this, however, not for the purpose of getting you to take sides against the hunting of kangaroos. I mention it to ask a question. When does the saving of any form of created life matter? When should I become involved? In the past, I sent a small amount of money to help save the Atlantic salmon from over-fishing. Also, I made a tiny contribution to help save the whales. As I mentioned in a previous sermon, I support the conservation of trout and trout streams. Maybe I'm just perverse about these things. I may be reacting to the macho men who must have handguns and wear camouflage clothing -- the kind who read magazines about mercenary soldiers and love watching Rambo. I admit my possible perversity. So now shall I spend a few minutes and a few dollars to save the kangaroos? Shall I write to the Australian government and tell them that I have canceled my plans to visit Australia (something I had not planned on doing anyway)? Shall I write to my congressman, urging legislation to ban kangaroo products? When does the saving of any form of created life matter? It was with that question that I wrestled on my walk that early August morning.

The answer at which I arrived was this: At some point, someone has to save those who cannot save themselves. At some point, someone must speak for those who cannot speak for themselves. At some point, someone has to enter the battle to save those who are deemed the "lesser breeds."

If kangaroos don't matter, then maybe other animals don't matter. If kangaroos don't matter, then maybe we don't need humane societies and laws regulating animal cruelty. Maybe we can let people have their cock fights and pit bull fights. Maybe we can forget about the people who sell kittens for live shark bait. Maybe we can forget about teaching our children kindness to their pets. Where do you draw the line for defining the limits of humane behavior?

If kangaroos don't matter, then maybe too there are lesser breeds of people. Maybe certain people can be the butt of our jokes. Maybe it doesn't matter if I use racist terms when telling jokes about persons of African, Polish, Jewish, Italian, or Oriental origin. Once, when I was discussing the Vietnam war with a businessman, he said to me, "You must remember that some people are just pawns in the great games of nations." He was speaking of Oriental people. He meant that it didn't matter if we dropped bombs on them. If kangaroos don't matter, then we can write off certain races of people and cultivate a lower level of outrage concerning the atrocities that are heaped upon them. If even a few American children were killed in an international incident, we would call for war. If the children of Soweto are being systematically starved, who cares?

Do you really want everyone in your heaven? Do you want that multitude out of every tribe and tongue and nation which is pictured in Revelation? Must everyone in heaven look like you and yours? Do you want the foreigners, the undesirables, the homeless, the addicts, and the gays to come home to our heavenly Father? Do you hope and pray and work for their homecoming? Do you love them unconditionally as Christ loves them unconditionally? And if you don't, how can you hope to be forgiven if you do not forgive others their debts? Heaven is for the forgiven and the forgiving. You see how much hangs upon my second question, "Are your enemies in your heaven?"

III - ARE THERE HORSES IN HEAVEN?

C. S. Lewis had an interesting idea about heaven. He believed that we could bring into heaven with us all of those with whom we will share the love of Christ. He offered the sanctified guess that the love of God is so boundless as to reach beyond human life into all of creation -- that God is utterly inclusive and unconditional in his love. As I mentioned earlier, the doors of the heavenly city are never shut.

Of course, that places the decision about horses in heaven with us. If God is utterly inclusive, you can lovingly bring into his presence any creature of God who will come with you. Finding a place for a horse in heaven is not a problem for God. His kingdom is very roomy. God can find room for another horse as easily as he can find room in his love for your worst enemy. So you can bring your horse or dog or cat, as long as you bring your enemy. Forgiving your enemy is no problem for a God of unconditional love. The forgiveness of our enemies is always our problem, not God's. If you cannot forgive your worst enemy and hope for their salvation, you do not and cannot know the love of Jesus. If you cannot share Christ's unconditional love with your enemy, you have rejected that unconditional love yourself. But if, in the love of Jesus, you will take the hand of your enemy and approach the open door of our heaven, you can bring every creature you have ever loved with you.

If your enemy does not choose to come, that is another problem. Your calling, as a forgiven sinner, is to live with the sanctified imagination that heaven is big enough to include any and all of God's creatures, including your worst enemies. If you can cultivate such compassionate imagination, all things are possible with God. Let me state it in another way.

Fourteen years ago next month, we were given our first horse, Ginger Snap. We had to leave her at our church conference center when we moved here to Pittsburgh. She will be 22 years old next month and can still run away with an inexperienced rider. Sometime thereafter, we bought our donkey, Hosanna. He will be about 20 years old this fall. It does not strain my imagination to believe I may meet them at the gates of heaven. Ginger has brought joy to hundreds of children. She will never act up when a child is on her back. At our Christmas Hand-in-Hand festival, Hosanna has brought joy to more than 100,000 visitors who have petted his nose. Many were handicapped and disabled. Both Ginger and Hosanna have served God's children faithfully. It will be no surprise to see them in heaven, along with our dogs -- Duchess, Scandal, Winston, Merlin, Sparky, and Churchill -- and also our cats -- Claude, Marmalade, Roasty Toasty, and Jeffrey -- plus a multitude of kittens born to them. They have brought simple, harmless joy to many hearts.

Likewise, it will be no surprise to find my worst enemies there. It may strain my imagination to picture them in heaven, but it does not strain my imagination to believe that Jesus loves them and finds beauty in them that I could never see.

The great surprise will be to find myself approaching those gates. I could never, in an eternity of time, feel worthy to draw near to those open gates of God's heaven. Only because of God's amazing grace would I dare draw near. Because of that grace -- and only because of that grace -- will I approach that open door. When I do, I hope that I will not be alone. I hope that I will have shared enough of Christ's love in this world to be able to bring many of his least, forgotten people and other creatures, great and small, with me.

❧

$\mathscr{R}$eflections Upon the Star of David

January 24, 1988

Scripture Lesson: **Hebrews 11 (Sections) and 12: 1, 2.**

❦

$\mathscr{T}$hank heaven for little girls! I guess I make that exclamation in a different spirit than it was made in song by Maurice Chevalier many years back in the movie, *Gigi.* As a father approaching the age of 60 and at the end of a decade in which I have watched my four children, one by one, leaving the nest, I find myself frequently saying, "Thank heaven for little girls and boys!" As one's own children move on and out, and as one who still has no grandchildren, I find myself glad at every occasion when little children give me even the smallest attention. Whether a little wave of the hand as they leave the chancel after the children's portion, or a short visit to my study to see my teddy bears, any small contact with children is most welcome.

For that and another reason, I was utterly surprised and delighted when, on the day before Christmas, the two little girls from across the street came to our front door with a gift of chocolate candy for me. I really don't know Lauren and Sarah that well, but ever since they moved in, we wave to one another and greet one another in our daily comings and goings. Their father shares with me a love of bicycling. Both our families have had the common experience of having a car stolen and returned, and we see one another's lights go on in the morning and off at night.

Lauren and Sarah had just finished celebrating the season of Hanukkah and were wearing outfits that they had been given during the observance of that Festival of Lights. They were beaming with delight as they presented me with my gift, and so I invited them in. They told me how they celebrated their season, and I showed them our two Christmas trees and took them up to my study to show them a small brass menorah which I keep on a shelf up there. A few days after Christmas, I brought them over here to the church to show them my teddy bear Christmas tree and took them into this sanctuary to let them stand in the pulpit. I gave each of them a tiny, hand-sized teddy bear, and we walked home, having completed our sharing of holiday customs.

There was another special reason for my delight with their visit. It was one that I could not share with them, but it gave a depth of meaning to their visit, which they will understand some day. Just the day before their visit, I had gone with two colleagues to an exhibition at the University of Pittsburgh. On exhibit were materials from the Auschwitz State Museum in Poland. After the first display at the United Nations during the winter of 1985-86, arrangements were made to carry the exhibition to major American cities.

I have read and preached about the Holocaust on numerous occasions. Although it is not a new subject for me, I am finding it difficult to describe the terrifying impact that one receives when viewing the materials and articles that have been preserved from that awful factory of death. There were photographs and copies of the deathly, cold correspondence that detailed the conception, planning, execution, and statistics of that nightmare of persecution. There were empty cans that had held the chemicals that released the Zyklon B poison gas, which could exterminate 2,000 victims at a time. There were the suitcases in which the victims packed their belongings, unaware of the destination of their journey. There were the shoes and other personal articles that were confiscated from them: the hair that was shaved off their heads to be used as upholstery material, the uniforms that some were given to wear, the yellow stars of David that marked them out as Jews, and the I.D. photographs of prisoners. Most moving were the photographs of the children.

And that is why one of my best Christmas presents this year was just the smiling faces of two little Jewish girls. Their radiance somehow said to me that the light and love of God cannot be extinguished by all of the world's darkness and hatred. I felt like shouting the opening words of my morning order of prayer, "Now blessed be the God of Israel, who only doeth wondrous things!" A few days later, in a New Year's reshuffling of the piles of books and papers in my home study, I found a yellow stained-glass star of David. I placed it in the window next to my desk where, maybe, Lauren and Sarah can see it. It will always remind me of Christmas 1987 and of the reflections that have been mine in the days since that week. Let me share them with you.

As I begin to do this, I am sure that someone is asking, "Why are you telling us all of this? We came to church to hear the gospel preached. We tune in on this radio broadcast to hear Biblical preaching. We don't want your humanistic opinions. What does Auschwitz have to do with the gospel of Jesus Christ?" Good question! Thanks for asking it, because it was the basic question asked by the Christians who stood by and allowed Auschwitz to happen.

Now there were many Christians who bravely resisted Hitler and the Holocaust. There is a considerable body of literature upon the subject of Christian resistance to Nazism (as well as about the indifference of many Christians). One of the theological documents in our Presbyterian Book of Confessions of which we should be very proud is the Theological Declaration of Barmen. As early as 1934, the Confessional Synod of the German Evangelical Church issued this defiant protest against Hitler's attempt to silence the church. In this declaration, Christians rejected the notion that the church should limit its activity to those areas of life defined as "spiritual" and that the state should order the rest of our life. Some of you also know that a brave, young German pastor, Dietrich Bonhoeffer, was executed for his participation in a plot to assassinate Hitler. Unfortunately, many Christians remained silent. They stood off at a safe distance, because they were asking the question, "What does Auschwitz have to do with the gospel of Jesus Christ?" Asking that question indicates that they did not know who Jesus really is -- and particularly, where he is.

THEY DID NOT KNOW THAT JESUS WAS IMPRISONED AT AUSCHWITZ

There were all kinds of prisoners at Auschwitz. There were political prisoners. There were Russian prisoners of war. There were Gypsies. There were thousands of homosexuals (identified as prisoners by a pink triangle), exterminated as "defectives." There were Christians. Mostly, there were Jews from Poland, Belgium, France, Greece, Holland, and Hungary. What many Christians did not know, and still do not know, is that Jesus was there. According to the parable in Matthew 25: 31-46, Jesus is always present where people are imprisoned and oppressed. To state that Jesus was at Auschwitz is therefore to make a Biblical statement and also a statement about the church's mission in the world, because the mission of the church is to be wherever Jesus is in the world.

We must rid ourselves of the absurd notion that Jesus Christ is the prisoner of the church. Many Christians harbor the unbiblical notion that the church is the principal residence of Jesus Christ, and that, wherever the church is, Jesus Christ is there. Jesus Christ is not wherever the church is. The church is wherever Jesus Christ is, and he does not limit himself to church buildings on Sunday mornings. He is not the private possession of the church, as though to suggest that the church decides when to "carry" him into the world. He is already in the world, and the mission of the church is to follow him, to be where Jesus is, and to become involved in his works of love and justice.

Please notice that I am talking about the church and not simply about the activity of Christians as individuals. In a recent superb sermon, our good neighbor at the First Presbyterian Church, Dr. Bruce Thielemann, exposed the absurdity of the notion that the mission of the church must be carried out principally by individuals and that the church must not speak and act as an institution. There is no guarantee that becoming a Christian will either make one sensitive to social evils or make one competent to deal with such evils. We wish that such were not the case, but witness the racism of the so-called "Bible Belt." Even if individual Christians were sensitive and competent to challenge the evils of the world, there aren't enough Christians to keep up with the problems of the world, because world population is growing faster than the church is growing. And if it be argued that the church must not speak or act upon matters in which we cannot reach unanimity, then let us recognize that, if we wait for the day of unanimity, we will never do anything. There is no unanimity about the meaning of the Bible, but still we preach and teach. There is no unanimity about evangelism and mission, but still we evangelize and send missionaries into the world. There is no unanimity about the evils and sufferings of society, but we must speak and act, because Jesus Christ is always imprisoned in the evils and sufferings of the world. Our mission is to be where Jesus is.

We cannot go as individuals into the Garfield neighborhood to deal with the suffering and deprivation there. The great majority of us are ill-equipped for such a mission, and even if we have such skills, we might not be welcome. But we can and are supporting street workers who are welcomed and who work effectively in that community. Because of their work, young people from that neighborhood enjoy the use of our gymnasium, and little children can be driven to our church to receive friendship and tutoring. This is something that we have to do as a church with other churches, and we are not doing it because we are better or smarter than people who live in Garfield, but because Jesus Christ is there, calling us to follow him and to make the difference that he can make in human life.

One can only wonder what a difference it might have made if more churches had followed Jesus in Nazi Germany. One wonders what we would have done under the circumstances. One wonders also what a difference it might make if the church would awaken to the Biblical fact that Jesus Christ is personally present and personally suffering in the sufferings of AIDS victims. Over against the hysteria of those who would build new concentration camps, the church must find some way to follow Jesus Christ in his healing compassion for all of his children.

Of course, there is no guarantee that the church will always speak and act correctly in its attempt to be with Jesus Christ in the world. Neither is there any guarantee that individual Christians will always conduct their discipleship correctly or effectively. However, our daily experience has certainly taught us that there is both strength and wisdom in decisions and actions undertaken in a concerted manner. The imperfection of our discipleship does not relieve us, either as a church or as individuals, of the responsibility to follow Jesus.

Jesus Christ is present wherever people suffer rejection, injustice, oppression, or sickness. The mission of the church is to be where he is. Those who let Auschwitz happen did not know that Jesus was imprisoned there.

THEY DID NOT KNOW THAT THEY WERE IMPRISONED AT AUSCHWITZ

There is no escape from the mercy and judgment of Jesus Christ. If we follow him in the world in his work of mercy, we will enjoy his mercy. If we will not go out to him and join him in his saving mission in the world, we bring his inescapable judgment upon ourselves. The worst victims of injustice are those who condone it. No one suffers from oppression as do those who are the oppressors.

Think of the terrible lostness of those who let it happen, helped it happen, and finally made it happen! It is no inconsiderable task to kill millions of people. It is one thing to have suffered as a prisoner, but consider the inevitable, inescapable spiritual darkness and unending misery of those who supplied the chemicals, those who manufactured the striped suits, those who built the buildings, those who did the plumbing, those who shaved the prisoners' heads -- let alone those who planned and did the killing. Could they ever be freed from the darkness and despair of their hardened conscience?

No one is ever free who disregards the suffering of others. Those who say there is no hunger in America are dying of a spiritual starvation that is separating them from God. Those who ignore the death squads of Central America are executing their own souls. Those who turn from the plight of the homeless will finally die the death of a frozen soul. If we do not follow Jesus Christ in his mission of mercy and salvation in the world, we are passing sentence upon ourselves, separating ourselves from him, and forfeiting the eternal freedom of our souls.

Faith in Jesus Christ, you see, is not some set of creedal terms or doctrinal shibboleths to which we give intellectual assent, nor some set of pious feelings that we are conditioned to enjoy by the mystique of religious sound effects. Faith is an intimate relationship in which we go where Jesus Christ goes, displaying his loving acceptance of all persons, and doing his works of mercy and justice. The only complete freedom that we can ever know as Christians is by such a life of faith and obedience to Jesus Christ.

A FINAL WORD

Thank heaven for little girls and for the reflections that they inspire. Our youngest, our little girl, Holly, left early this morning to take up residence in California and to seek her fortune there. To get started, she will live with her brother, Dwight, in Los Angeles and work at something until her plans for graduate school are fully formed. We will miss her, but are proud that she is courageous enough to leave home. Leaving home is the proof of successful parenting, I guess.

She doesn't have a car yet, but she took the women's liberation bumper sticker that she will attach to the car that she plans to purchase out there. I don't think Holly will ever go too far wrong if she lives by what that sticker says. If she understands and lives out her faith in Jesus Christ in terms of that bumper sticker, I think I will always be proud of her. It reads simply, "No one is free when others are oppressed."

The Likeness of Christ

April 10, 1988

*Scripture Lesson: **John 20: 11-18, 24-31.***

Toward the end of this past Lenten season, I was the speaker at a men's communion breakfast at one of the churches in our Pittsburgh Presbytery. The meal was prepared and served by the women of the church, and one of the women working in the kitchen was evidently a regular listener to our radio broadcast service. Familiar with my voice, but not with my face, before the program began, this lady called the pastor aside and inquired of him which one of the men at the speaker's table was Morgan Roberts. When the pastor pointed toward the one with thinning, graying hair, wearing a dark gray preacher's suit, and a regimental stripe red and black tie, she exclaimed, "O my! He doesn't look like he's supposed to look!" Of course, I was not at all surprised. No Welshman ever looks as good as his voice sounds!

Her comment set me thinking about the question with which we will start out today.

What is a minister supposed to look like?

For that matter, what is a Christian supposed to look like?

There is often a defective theology in some of the simple gospel hymns that I learned when I first became a Christian. Still, many of them have deep roots in my spiritual soil, and I find no reason to uproot them. (They are vastly preferable to the lightweight lyrics of the glitzy gospel according to Hollywood, which prevails in fundamentalist/ evangelical television nowadays.) In one of those gospel songs from my teenage years, there was the repetitive refrain, "I would be like Jesus!"

Simple theology, yes! But that aspiration does have some Biblical basis, because we are promised that ". . . when he appears we shall be like him, for we shall see him as he is." Perhaps then, I must begin my quest for my proper ministerial identity by asking what Jesus is supposed to look like in my mind.

WHAT IS JESUS SUPPOSED TO LOOK LIKE?

Christians seem to have varying degrees of interest in that question. Some branches of the Christian family have produced more artistic likenesses of Christ than others. In our own Presbyterian/Reformed tradition, there has been a certain fear of the temptations to idolatry that can arise from reliance upon the images and likenesses that are employed in religious art. For many years, our places of worship were sternly barren. The sanctuary of the first church that I served contained neither cross nor candles. There was a strain of Scottish Covenanter blood in that congregation, and when we relocated to another sanctuary and placed a Celtic cross and candles on a gradin shelf above the communion table, one of the older members remarked to me that it had always been her impression that we had gone through the Reformation to get rid of those idolatrous objects.

On the other hand, other branches of the Christian family have believed that we need as many images as possible to keep faith vivid. Whenever I was in the homes of my Roman Catholic relatives on my father's side of the family, I would be reminded of how, not only in their places of worship, but also in their homes, religious art had an important function. Perhaps it was not great art, but those visual reminders of the sacred heart of Jesus and of the Blessed Virgin Mary kept alive the call to a sacrificial and holy life.

Of course, not all Protestants are as dour and severe as Presbyterians. There are probably many Baptist and Methodist homes in which one can find some likeness of Jesus. Even if it is some ghastly saccharine portrait, it may keep faith vivid and serve as a reminder of the Christian commitment of the family.

However, whatever the tradition of religious art in which you were nurtured, I am wondering if you live your daily life with some likeness of Jesus implanted in your mind. When you sing hymns of praise, read the gospels, or say your prayers, do you operate with some picture of him in your mind? Is it some dear likeness of him from the friendly art of your Sunday School days? Or was it implanted by some picture of him that hung in the home of your childhood? Or are there several likenesses that you have of Jesus? Some people even keep some favorite likeness of Jesus before them when they offer their morning or evening prayers.

A dear lady told me once that she could visualize Jesus in much of her daily life, but especially when she could be in the countryside, where she could picture him walking through the fields. I think I envy anyone whose upbringing has provided them with such lovely imagery, because I don't think that I have any mental images of Jesus that come to me when I read the gospels or offer my prayers. Maybe that is why the 20th chapter of John means so much to me. In that chapter, I find two clues to the likeness of Christ. That last lovely look at our living Lord, which is given to us in the Gospel of John, reminds me that he is a **plain man** and a **wounded man.**

The living Jesus is a plain man. When Mary first saw the risen Jesus, she did not recognize him; she supposed that he was the gardener. There's a priceless commentary upon the mighty resurrection of our Lord! In contrast to the cruel conquerors of the world who, in their moments of triumph, are painted in gaudy colors of ruthless super-power, God's victory is the raising of his son to our plain, common humanity. This conquering hero emerges from the tomb simply as an ordinary working man. Thus, as the risen Jesus ascends into heaven, we are left with the assurance that there is an ordinary human seated in heaven at the right hand of God the Father Almighty. The all-powerful Lord who has broken the bars of death and ascended into the presence of God is a plain man!

The living Jesus is also a wounded man. The disciples and Thomas are convinced when they see the wounds in his hands and on his side. The resurrection has not removed the mark of the nails and the scar of the spear. Even in his heavenly glory, Jesus wears those wounds as badges of victory. So therefore, we can also say that there is man a with scars seated at the right hand of God the Father Almighty.

So that's what Jesus is supposed to look like: a plain man and a wounded man.

SO WHAT AM I SUPPOSED TO LOOK LIKE?

I am wondering what the lady in the church kitchen thought I was supposed to look like. My guess is that I probably would like to have the looks that she expected me to have. I would like to have more hair, a more finely shaped nose, better vision (so that I could see without these thick glasses), and an adjusted metabolism that would allow me to eat all that I want without gaining weight. That's what I would like to look like.

However, if I am called to look like my Lord, **I am called to be a plain man.** But of course, just how plain is plain? In these times of extensive hunger and homelessness, there are certain deeply committed Christians who are trying to live in simpler lifestyles as their witness to God's demand for love and justice in the world. But then again, just how simple is simple?

A recent book by David E. Shi, *In Search of the Simple Life,* traces the history of various religious groups that have been committed to a plain and simple style of living. As one might guess, such groups have a history of splinterization. At first, every one is in agreement about the standard of simplicity. However, after a while, some faction wants to liberalize the rules, while another group wants to make the standards more demanding.

Reading through an Amish document written as late as 1950, I discovered an extensive definition of just what constitutes plain living. It discussed the proper appearance of clothing, hair, furniture, horse-drawn carriages, stoves, and household items, and sought to define just how plain is plain, right down to the question of plain suspenders without buckles. However, that's just one group's definition. Such different practices within groups dedicated to the simple life reflect the difficulty for any religious group in defining simplicity.

Presbyterians engage in the same discussions, but not openly. We do not put our debates into print, but we probably engage in some inner questions and judgments about those of our number who appear to be living too extravagantly on the one hand, or perhaps too self-righteously simple on the other hand. Our cars, our clothes, and our clubs become subjects of inner questioning as we wrestle with the question of how plain is plain.

Although that question can never be settled satisfactorily in a group setting, I must settle it for myself as I profess to follow a plain Lord. Let me share with you an approach that has helped me.

Instead of beginning with a definition of the outward appearance of my life, the quest for my plain and simple self in Christ must grow from the inner core of my life. In such an inward search, I find certain questions to be helpful.

- Can I live without pretense?
- Can I live without pretending to know something about every thing, as though having all the answers?
- Can I live without pretending to be somebody superior and more important than others?
- Can I live without whining and complaining, as though my problems give me the exclusive right to harbor some special grudge against the management of the universe?
- Can I speak the plain truth in both kindness and candor?
- Can I live without the pretense of being perfect, admit when I'm wrong, ask for forgiveness when I have failed, and seek help when I have fallen?
- Can I be honest enough to laugh at myself when I do something stupid and to shed real tears when I hurt?
- Can I live without demanding recognition, remembering that my risen Lord was not recognized at the very moment of his triumph?
- Can I dare to be just plain Morgan?

Knowing that there is nothing that makes me more special than anyone else in all of the world -- not my car, my clothes, my club, my job, nor the house I live in -- and that my only real specialness arises from my being a sinner saved by the death of a man who looked like a gardener, can I learn to live without pretense?

If I am called to look like my Lord, I am called to be a plain man.

I am also called to be a wounded man.

Paul said that he bore on his body the marks of Jesus. I suppose he meant the scars of the hardships and sufferings that he had borne for the sake of the gospel. As of this date, there are no marks of suffering on my body. There's a small scar on my left elbow, sustained in a bad fall in a bicycle race in which I was attempting to raise money for the hungry by betting my congregation that I could beat all of the teenagers in our church in a 30-mile race. I don't think that that scar will count as a real mark of suffering, because I was having too much fun trying to win the bet.

Think of the bruises of beauty that the saints and martyrs will wear as the royal jewels of heaven -- the marks of the hangman's rope, the scars from being burned at the stake, the gashes of the lion's jaws, and the burns and bullet wounds of modern day martyrs. Whether or not we will see such marks, I do not know. Maybe we will, because the risen Jesus still bore the scars of his sufferings. Whether or not we do, it helps me to visualize such a scene, because there I will stand, with hands beautifully soft and unblemished, before one whose heavenly diadem is still that crown of thorns. How shall I dare to place my hand in his pierced hand of welcome, if I have no scar? Amy Carmichael writes,

Hast thou no scar?
No hidden scar on foot, or side, or hand?
I hear thee sung as mighty in the land,
I hear them hail thy bright ascendant star,
Hast thou no scar?

No wound? no scar?
Yet, as the Master shall the servant be,
And pierced are the feet that follow me;
But thine are whole: can he have followed far
Who has nor wound nor scar?

We cannot all be martyrs, but we can have wounded hearts. We can be bent under secret burdens that we decide to carry for his name's sake. We can bleed internally by silent suffering that we learn to accept for his honor. We can be worn away with arduous labors that we perform cheerfully for the advancement of his kingdom. Surely, he will see those secret scars on that day and recognize us as those who have followed him. Indeed, some plain living and sacrificial giving for his sake can produce a few faint wounds by which he will be able to know that we have been identified with him in the fellowship of his sufferings.

For that matter, becoming a plain and wounded people has become a matter of present urgency here on earth. A hurting world does not need preachers with stripes on their sleeves as much as it needs shepherds with stripes on their hearts. A suffering world cries out for a church that will speak more eloquently by its wounds than by its words. Such a world seeks a church that looks like its Lord, who was mistaken for a gardener and who, upon closer examination, was found to be a wounded man.

In this day in which the resurrection of Jesus has been falsely interpreted as a symbol of success which gives some preachers the mandate to build great kingdoms for themselves and to preach a gospel of prosperity, we need to remember that our Jesus was raised to a plain and wounded life. God's objective in raising Jesus from the dead was not to supply us with the power to think successfully, but to give us courage to be ordinary people in a world of pride and pretense. The plain and wounded risen Jesus is God's idea of an authentic human being, and that is what we're supposed to look like!

What Next?

....

January 1, 1989

*Scripture Lesson: **Luke 2: 21-40.***

❦

COMMENTS ON THE LESSON

*W*ere it not for the author of the Gospel of Luke, we would know nothing of the two characters, Simeon and Anna, who appear ever so briefly as the curtains are about to fall upon Luke's nativity narrative. If we try to envision the story of Jesus' birth as the first act of a play, then there seems to be a certain artistry in bringing these two characters on stage just at this moment. With the focus of attention having been upon a young mother and her baby, there is an engaging contrast in the entrance of two very old people who speak of this child in such a way as to prepare us for what is coming in the rest of the play.

Both are older people. Simeon's age is not given, but he has been clinging to the promise that he will not see death until his eyes have looked upon the promised Christ. His song of gratitude for the fulfillment of this promise, the Nunc Dimittis, breathes a note of relief and suggests his willingness to depart this life, now that the promise has been fulfilled. Anna's age is, at least, 84. Both are painted as deeply pious and prophetic persons. Anna is called a prophetess, and Simeon is described as one upon whom the Holy Spirit rests and through whom the Spirit speaks.

Their piety, however, is not the stereotypical spirituality of older folk who have nothing left to do but be religious in a backward direction, but the vigorous and energizing faith of those who live thrusting themselves forward with the future. Seen as such, they set the stage for what will follow in the entire two-volume work that is comprised by Luke/Acts. Across the span of both books, the main characters will lead liberated lives, carried forward by the Holy Spirit toward that future that God is ever unveiling.

SERMON

"What next?" I can't remember any announced sermon title that has ever drawn forth so much advanced comment from the members of my staff or the members of my family. There is a reason for their early interest in what this sermon might be about, because anyone who has to live with me on a regular basis comes to know with what frequency that expression crosses my lips in daily conversation. I wonder how many of you use it with something of the same regularity as I do, and I wonder what kinds of meanings you impart to it as you use it as a question or as an exclamation.

Oftentimes, I notice that it is used not at all as a question which invites an answer, but as an expression of minor frustration. Especially as we get on in life and are confronted by bewildering changes over which we may have little control, we may ask, "What next?" Several years ago, when I used it in such a manner in the presence of my predecessor, Bob Holland, to express my mild exasperation about some foolish fashion in the church business, he told me of a similar setting in which he had heard it from an elder in a small church in Scotland. In this little church, where it had never been the custom for the choir to wear robes, a new pastor had been instrumental in finding a contributor who provided the funds for robing the choir. Being of an older, anti-catholic disposition, this elder viewed such an innovation as a sure slide toward popish ways and said to Bob, "What next?"

In such a setting, the term becomes a statement of helpless frustration about those changes in the world over which we feel we have little or no control. We almost breathe the words, expecting no answer other than some expression of sympathy from a fellow sufferer. During her last years, my mother even came to speak of the weather in such terms, especially if bad weather fell upon the day when I was to take her to her senior adult Fifty-and-Up Club sponsored by our church in Michigan. Until she was 94, she attended this club meeting with regularity. With the hired help of one of our custodians, we would carry her down the stairs and out to the car, strapped in a stretcher chair. At church, we would lift her into a wheelchair in which she would remain until the program was over, after which we would reverse the process, and take her home. In winter weather, when snow and ice covered our walkway, it simply was not safe to attempt this carrying procedure, and she would have to miss the meeting. All that afternoon I would hear her on the phone, describing the weather as a kind of conspiracy that proved that something must be wrong with the government in Washington. Speaking of the snow and ice, she would say, "It's terrible what's happening! What next?"

With the minor or major frustrations of each day, I suppose many of us utter this question, or some equivalent expression, to help relieve the weight of life's small or large burdens. However, I notice that I use it also in an almost entirely opposite sense to express delight in the accomplishments or inventions that brighten our life.

When I learn of some new program that can be installed in my computer to make writing or record keeping a faster or more efficient process, I express my elation with the marvels of the modern world by saying, "What next?"

In somewhat this same way, I find that I use this phrase to express happy amazement with the accomplishments of little children. When they show me what new thing they have learned, or what marvelous invention they have put together, I whisper with quiet appreciation, "What next?" Once when I used it to express delight in the singing talents of a little boy, he stared at me in bewilderment and answered, "I don't know what's next!" After listening to three more songs from his repertoire, I again exclaimed, "What next?" This time, with even greater befuddlement, he stated, "I told you, I don't know what's next!"

On this first day of a new year, I suggest that we listen again to this little boy's answer. With childlike, heavenly wisdom, he is content with not knowing what is next.

FAITH OFFERS US NO CONTROLLING KNOWLEDGE
OF THE FUTURE

Surely, there are those who look forward to a coming year with something more than the minor frustration with which I frequently ask, "What next?"

Some people have endured all that they can endure of personal loss, so that, as they ask what is next, they wonder how much more they can possibly endure. Some people ask that question, no longer hoping for relief, but wondering if they could just understand why it is they have had to endure such "outrageous fortune." Still others, though not suffering from what they have experienced along a road going nowhere, would like some clue for finding a better road that they might follow, a road that might be going somewhere.

The deepest faith in Jesus Christ will not supply full and final answers to such questions.

Faith offers us no answers amidst the natural disasters of life. Thousands of our Armenian sisters and brothers would like to know why. A kind of quasi-religious reasoning can point to the overriding and general reliability of nature, or even to the outpouring of compassion and the uniting of the human family in such disasters. But to those who suffer real loss, such reasoning must seem cruel and cold. No answer is given.

No full and final answer is given to us in the personal disasters of life. We can often trace some root cause for personal problems back to bad choices in which we disobeyed God's laws for human life. Even that kind of reasoning has left many sincere souls burdened with unearned guilt. But what of those instances in which we have followed the will of God as conscientiously as we could and still found ourselves on a path that ended on a cross? Indeed, is not the tormenting question of our crucified Lord who had lived in perfect obedience -- is not his cry ("My God, my God, why...?" Mark 15: 34) the very word that shakes the foundations of all religious certainty? No answer is given.

And yet, our greed for controlling knowledge of the future fuels the fortunes of those who have made a big business of selling the counterfeit religion of certainty:

- Their answers may be attractively packaged as formulas for successful Christian living, which guarantee, if not the best decisions, at least some peace in our being certain that we are right in a world in which all the others are wrong.
- Or their answers may take the form of intricate maps and charts, which reveal the true meaning of Bible prophecy so that, armed with a timetable telling us where the course of the entire world is headed, smugly watching these cosmic events unfolding, we can enjoy the same superiority over others. One radio evangelist has even established an investment counseling service for true believers that is grounded in the true meaning of Bible prophecy! How will PaineWebber ever compete with such an offering?
- Moving farther out toward the edge are those sad seers who by the stars can chart our futures, as well as those who would call back the dead to give us some daily direction.

What religious faith is there in simply knowing what the future holds? Chastising those who would call back the dead to know the shape of the future, George MacDonald asked, "Is that to worship God? It is no more religion than the belief that the sun will rise tomorrow is religion." Religion is not the business of obtaining knowledge about the future. To have such knowledge would relieve us from having to live by faith. To desire such knowledge is the fallen hunger for the forbidden fruit that would make us like God and render us superior to the rest of the human family. Idolatrous greed may hunger for such certainty -- genuine faith will never!

What next? To ask that is to ask the wrong question, a question that the Bible will not answer. Biblical faith never tells us **what** is next; it only tells us **who** is next, and in giving that answer, it is very brief. From the silent heavens over the cradle and the cross comes only the answer -- in the end, God.

It is easy to miss that main point in our reading of the Bible. The Bible does talk about the future, but when it does, it speaks not to our curiosity, but offers a call for commitment. The Bible talks of the future only to assure us that God will meet us at every moment of the future, and that, on every tomorrow, he will be calling us into a renewed relationship. Biblical faith offers us no other answer for our daily life than the person of Jesus Christ.

Christianity is uniquely person-centered, calling for a commitment in faith and love to the person of Jesus Christ. To offer any answer for the future, other than this personal relationship with him, is to abandon the life of faith and to betray his sole lordship of the future. When we know him as savior, friend, and lord, we know all that we need to know about what is next. He, and he alone, is next.

When I know that Jesus Christ is the only one in my future, I can know a quality for living that can never be supplied by the various practitioners of Christianized magic. Knowing that he is the end of all things means that he is not only at the end of all things, but also at the end of every moment. He is always waiting to meet me in the next moment or in the next person. Living life in his presence is like living every moment at that point in the fairy tale when the clock is about to strike midnight, when something exciting is about to happen. Instead of living backward, I can live a forward life in the presence of the Lord, who is the end of all things.

As Luke's two-volume story sets the infant Jesus on his way with the blessing of Simeon and Anna (both forward looking people), it comes to its conclusion (Acts 28: 31) with a picture of Paul who, though imprisoned, is "preaching the kingdom of God and teaching about the Lord Jesus Christ quite openly and unhindered." Such open and unhindered living is the quality of life in every moment for those who know that Jesus Christ stands in every next moment. They never ask "What next?," because they know who waits to meet them in every tomorrow. There are all kinds of things that we do not need to know when we live in the presence of the eternal now with Jesus Christ.

A FINAL WORD

Let me credit a former teacher, Professor John R. Bodo, for the kernel of the thought with which I end this sermon. Six years ago this week, our David's dear Boxer, Winston, died of cancer. It is a Christmas that we will never forget. Still, his memory is kept alive by the very active presence of his nephew, Churchill, who is my constant companion, and who sat at my feet as I wrote this sermon. (Even though he was Sally's gift to me, she maintains that he is the most ill-behaved animal in all of dogdom.)

Churchill is unceasingly at my side. He waits outside the glass door of the shower when I bathe. He exists to be in my presence. This does not mean that he understands what is going on in my mind, or why I leave him to go to church, or why I feed him in a certain way or take him for a walk at one time and not at another. As with God and man, so it is with man and dog: my ways are higher than his ways, and my thoughts are beyond the reach of his thoughts. Still, he probably thinks that I exist for the sole purpose of caring for him and spending time with him, just as I often think that God's principal business is that of listening to me and taking care of me.

Churchill has no answers about why I let certain things happen to him. I am sure he cannot understand why I let the veterinarian stick needles in him. Still, he jumps in the car with enthusiasm when I invite him to make that annual trip for the needle sticking. He does not know it, but someday I will have to take him to the vet for the last time. He will not know what is happening to him, nor why it is happening. He lives without answers. However, his is the bliss of the eternal now, and on that last day, he will drive to the vet's knowing what he has always known: *he knows whose dog he is, and he knows whom he loves.* Creatures who know that can live without answers -- without having to ask, "What next?"

$\mathcal{T}$he Wild Flag

October 1, 1989

Scripture Lesson: **I Corinthians 11: 23-26, II Peter 3: 1-11.**

$\mathcal{I}$n the 1943 Christmas issue of *The New Yorker* magazine, E. B. White (known to most of us as the author of such classic children's stories as *Charlotte's Web* and *Stuart Little*) shared with his readers a rather extraordinary dream. It is all the more extraordinary when one considers that this dream came to him in 1943, before the formation of the United Nations organization (for that matter, even before the Dumbarton Oaks conference which was preliminary to the U.N.), and almost two years before the advent of nuclear weapons at Hiroshima, therefore long before the time when people began speculating about the nuclear holocaust of a third world war.

In his sleep, there came to him this dream of a conference of all nations, following the devastation of a third world war. Following this holocaust, there were only about 200 people left on the face of the earth. Still, the delegates from the remaining 83 countries gathered to discuss the possibilities of a lasting peace. Each delegate brought the flag of his/her homeland, except the delegate from China (which, at that date, was not yet a Communist country).

The Chinese delegate arrived carrying a shoebox, which contained a wildflower that looked very much like an iris. When asked why he had not brought his nation's flag, he said that he had discussed the matter with one of his few surviving Chinese countrymen (who happened to be an old sage) and that they had concluded that they would no longer have a cloth flag for China. His proposal was that all nations adopt this wildflower as their wild flag. When asked about his reasoning, he said that the flower was beautiful and could be grown everywhere on the earth. If we all adopted it, he said, we would no longer be able to insult one another's flags.

Immediately, the delegates began objecting. One said that it could not be waved. To this objection, the Chinese delegate replied that it was more beautiful at rest or when simply stirred by a gentle breeze. Another said that it was too gentle a symbol, and that it would leave him feeling that he no longer belonged to the master race. To this, the Chinese delegate observed that the master race, along with the human race, was now virtually extinct.

The most interesting objection was advanced by the delegate from Patagonia, who said that he feared that such a wild flag would be an unpopular idea. "It will, undoubtedly," sighed the Chinese delegate. "But now that there are only a couple of hundred people on earth, even the word 'unpopular' loses most of its meaning. At this juncture we might conceivably act in a sensible, rather than a popular, manner." At this point, he produced 82 more shoeboxes, giving a wild flag to each delegate. On the next day, the conference ended, and the delegates went home, ". . . marveling at what they had accomplished in so short a time."

I don't know whether or not E. B. White actually had this dream, or whether, like John Bunyan, some trace of dream material inspired a story that was related in story form as though it had been a complete dream. However it may have arisen in White's imaginative mind, it is a rather extraordinary fantasy, considering the way that it predated those events and circumstances that set the world wondering about how we might live together in a world which, literally, has the capability of destroying itself. What is interesting is the manner in which dreams often provide us with those insights and visions that inspire the wisdom and strength by which we face the most difficult challenges of life.

As we come to the holy table of our Lord on this World Communion Sunday, I want you to consider the fact that the earliest New Testament explanation of the Lord's Supper presents it to us as a meal that feeds a dream.

That's one truth about the sacrament of Holy Communion that we often overlook. Obviously, the Lord's Supper bids us to look backward upon the death of Christ. At our communion services, we often select hymns that can also appropriately be sung at Good Friday services. While this is true, this backward-looking, memorial orientation is reversed when we come to the last phrase of the words of institution. We partake of this holy meal as a way of bearing witness to the saving death of Jesus "until he comes."

It is clear that the first generation of New Testament Christians, along with the Apostle Paul himself, believed that the return of Christ was going to happen in their own lifetime. Although they were wrong, as well as disappointed, in this hope, it is also clear that the second and third generation of New Testament Christians held on to this hope. They accepted the fact that the Lord's return had been delayed, but they did not give up their hope in the eventual return of Christ and the establishment of his kingdom.

Because of this, there are certain images of the primitive church that we ought to keep in our minds whenever we celebrate this sacrament. I suppose that, whenever we come to communion, it is impossible for us not to think of the various sanctuaries in which we have made our communions. I certainly do. I think back upon my first church and the heavy mahogany table, placed at floor level below a central pulpit and surrounded by chairs for the elders -- exquisite antiques upholstered with black horsehair. Or I may remember the openness and lightness of the chancel in the modern Georgian sanctuary of my Michigan church with its "high altar" effect. All of you have memories and images such as these, which come to you when we celebrate the Lord's Supper. Still, when those words of institution are read, we need to remember those primitive Christians who had no sanctuaries and who slipped away to secret places to have their communion. According to Paul, they were not the big people in their community; they were neither powerful nor noble. Thus, when they ate this bread and drank this cup, they were reminded that a day was coming when God's kingdom of love and justice would be built in this world. It was not of a "heaven up there" of which they dreamed; instead, just as they had been taught by Jesus to pray "thy kingdom come, thy will be done on earth" -- even so this holy meal taught them to wait and work for the coming of the king and the kingdom. This meal fed and sustained that hope.

So when we come to this sacrament, we must never think of it as our quiet, sequestered place of retreat from the world. Quite the opposite -- this meal represents the beachhead that God has established in a God-rejecting world. And from this point, nourished and sustained by hope, we go forth to work in the world those works which make for peace and to do battle with all of those forces and values that deny God's love and justice.

Ten years before E. B. White shared his dream about the wild flag with his readers, another expression of extraordinary world vision took place in this sanctuary. This vision was all the more extraordinary because of the events that darkened the mood of our country and world back in 1933. The nation was still recovering from the Great Depression, and on the world stage, Hitler had become German Chancellor. Books by non-Nazi and Jewish authors were being burned. Jewish artists and intellectuals were fleeing for their life, and the first concentration camps were, without widespread public knowledge, being erected. In such a day, Shadyside's pastor, Hugh Thomson Kerr, conceived the idea of gathering all the churches of Christendom together on one designated Sunday of the year for the observance of a World-Wide Communion Sunday.

It began here in this sanctuary, and its beginning is memorialized on that brass plate in the center of the marble chancel floor. That marker, interestingly, is set within an inlaid marble design in the shape of a compass. As Dr. Holland once observed, hardly ever does one find the compass employed as a symbol in Christian architecture. However, such was the world vision of Dr. Kerr, and it was thoroughly consistent with the most ancient tradition surrounding the celebration of the Lord's Supper.

Since the days of the primitive church, this sacrament has been observed as a common meal, which looks not only backward to the upper room that climaxed Jesus' first advent, but also forward to his coming again to recreate a new world in which righteousness dwells. This holy table commits us to something beyond the narrow agenda of any one nation; it commits us to that larger kingdom of love and justice that Jesus Christ will bring to earth for all of God's children.

While it is undeniable that only God's power can bring in that kingdom and save the world from itself, it is equally unthinkable that God's people, as they watch and wait for that kingdom, can remain silent and complacent in the face of any and every evil power that thwarts the dream of such a kingdom. Those who celebrate this meal, which proclaims the redeeming love of Christ "until he comes," cannot be tolerant toward those whose limited vision obstructs or hinders the cause of peace. Those who pray "Thy kingdom come" cannot stand with those guilty bystanders whose silent complicity allows evil to reign.

To come to the Lord's table is not an act of private, personal piety, as much as it is a commitment to prophetic courage. It demands that we find every possible way to say to the world that it is high time to turn from speeches that echo popular prejudice and engage in prophetic and effective actions that are sensible.

There is something wonderfully commonplace about the table that stands at the center of the church's worship. It has something to say about the down-to-earth, sensible agenda of the church, and it sets the tone of our message to the world. It calls us to cry out for the simple needs of all God's people who need more bread, and not more guns; more homes, and not more prisons to house the next generation of convicts who are being malformed in the hovels of homelessness; more beds for those who are old and ill, and not more lounging places in the sunbelt for the idle rich.

The hope of our Lord's coming again calls us away from the popular wisdom of a fallen, God-rejecting world, and commits us to those simple, sensible lifestyles and agendas that anticipate the coming of God's new earth in which his righteousness dwells. It is that commitment that we renew as we come to the Lord's table on this special day of world-wide communion.

> *Now to your table, Lord, your people come;*
> *We seek your face.*
> *Hung'ring and thirsting, longing for our home;*
> *Grant us your grace!*
> *Your bread and wine our famished souls will feed;*
> *Your loving presence fill our deepest need.**

* *This one-verse communion hymn was written by Dr. Roberts to be sung by choir and congregation as the elders of the church came to the communion table. Written in 1988, it was sung to the tune Sandon.*

Richer For His Presence

June 17, 1990

*Scripture Lesson: **Philippians 4: 4-9.***

I suppose that, although today is designated liturgically as the Second Sunday after Trinity, the fact that it is Father's Day has more meaning to most of my listeners. Let me therefore begin with some material which, though it is not 'father' material, is at least something close to 'grandfather' material.

Sometime several years ago, I told you about a little boy in my Michigan congregation who, because his grandparents lived far away, adopted me as his local grandfather and invited me to come to his elementary school on grandparents' day. From the last photograph that I received, this adopted grandson, Paul Bunting, is no longer a little boy; he appears to be taller than I am. Shortly before we left Michigan, one of our most prolific female cats, Sari, had one of her many litters. With his parents' permission, Paul was allowed to pick out a kitten which would, in a sense, be a symbol of our continuing relationship. As might be guessed, he named it Morgan. (Interestingly, other kittens which, from time to time, we have given away have been given the same distinctive name.)

Not too long ago, I received the following letter from Kelly and Jessie Bunting, Paul's two younger sisters:

"Dear Mr. Roberts,

Morgan has just died. We had to put him to sleep. He had diabetes and cancer. Everybody is very sad. Is Morgan's mother still alive and does she still have kittens? Jessie and I would like another black kitten. No cat will ever beat Morgan. We all really miss him.

> *Your friend,*
> *Kelly Bunting"*

Well, what shall I tell them? It would be interesting to pass out sheets of writing paper and let each of you compose an appropriate reply. There are informal churches in which the preachers engage in such exercises, posing some question for deliberation, assigning the task of writing an answer, reading the various replies with some brief comment, and letting all of that be the morning sermon. Such a substitute kind of discussion sermon would probably not fly well in Shadyside Church; however competent you may be in giving good answers to spiritual, moral, or ethical questions, I know that you expect me to prove to you that I have spent some time preparing some utterance of substance.

So, let me tell you what I think needs to be said. I will not phrase it in the language of children, but I will, throughout this sermon, talk somewhat about animals. If you are a good listener, you will realize that I am talking about much more than animals. And if you don't think that talking about animals is a proper way of expressing Christian truth, let me remind you that some of the most profound God-talk in our generation was brought off by C. S. Lewis in his Narnia tales, in which he talked about God by talking about animals.

Let me offer two ideas:

No one (or no thing or no activity) can ever replace someone with whom you have enjoyed a loving relationship. Whether it be a father, mother, brother, sister, spouse, child, friend, lover, dog or cat -- when a truly loving relationship comes to an end, we must learn to say, as these two little girls have already learned, "No cat will ever beat Morgan."

We live in a world in which all loving relationships are brought to some kind of an ending at some time. The circumstances may vary, but no relationship is forever; and when the end comes, we will never be able to replace that creature of God, person or animal, by whom such happiness has been brought into our lives. That's the way the world works, and mature people, of any faith, will learn to accept such endings courageously. They will not go about acting as though they were the only person in the history of the world who has lost a loved one.

It is, of course, tempting to believe that we can find some substitute for the one whom we have lost. There is a popular wisdom that says that, when the old cat dies, we should go right out the next day to the Animal Rescue League to select a new kitten. I do not personally endorse such an approach, but I confess that I have often been tempted to believe that there are animal substitutes.

Long before I came to be your pastor, in a sermon which I preached from this pulpit, I told you about the death of Winston, a grand and noble Boxer who was the inseparable companion of our oldest son, David. To my dying day, I will never forget the night Winston left us. Several years later, David left us to go and work in Germany. Although it would be for only a few months, it was very difficult for me to say good-bye to David. One month after he was gone, Sally went out and found a Boxer puppy, who had been sired by Winston's sire, and brought him home as a surprise birthday present. In a way, it fulfilled the very need which little Kelly and Jessie feel: to have a kitten related to Morgan. However, this new Boxer puppy, whom we named Churchill, did not fill the vacant place left by Winston. Instead, Churchill made and filled his own place. In no way could Churchill diminish the memory or loss of Winston; he was just another different and wonderfully loving animal companion, and now that Churchill is gone (he died in December), no one can take his place.

Advertisers of certain products often warn us, "Beware of substitutes!" It is good advice, but we need to remember that, in human relationships, the substitutes can be very subtle. There are all kinds of compensatory and compulsive behaviors in which we may engage in our vain attempt to keep alive a human relationship that God, in his wisdom, has brought to an end. However, if we learn to refuse the substitutes, we can learn to live with the good pain of knowing that we enjoyed a truly loving relationship with someone unique -- so unique that they can never be replaced.

And when we simply accept this good pain, refusing the anesthetizing effect of false substitutes and substitute behaviors, our eyes will begin to be open to the uniqueness of other people who are still in our lives. Every day God surrounds us with all kinds of people who are one of a kind. We are having our one chance to enjoy them and to learn why God has brought them into our lives. When our time with them is over, no one will be able to fill their place. If we spend all of today trying to keep yesterday's relationships alive, we will miss the new loving relationships that God wants us to enjoy today.

When a daughter or son says to me of their dear departed father, "I don't know how I'll ever stop missing him," my answer is, "Who ever said you were supposed to? No one will ever take his place; miss him as much as you want and get on with your life today." No cat will ever beat Morgan, and there'll never be another Winston, just like there'll never be another Churchill. However, we still have Sparky, and Sasha, and Sari, and Bear; and they're all one of a kind, just like all of the people whom God has kept alive for some reason and who are still a vital and unique part of our life today.

No one (or no thing or no activity) can ever replace someone with whom you have enjoyed a loving relationship. Indeed, no one needs to replace those whom we have loved and lost, because they already have an enduring place in our world.

When I say this, I am not saying that our only eternal life is in the memory of others. For today, we're not talking about the subject of the life eternal, so don't misinterpret my words as though they were meant to suggest that an enduring memory constitutes our only life after death. For that matter, I am not talking about memory as much as I am talking about something else: character. *Good character is the only thing that we can leave behind us as our constructive contribution to the world.*

My Biblical justification for saying this is found in the statement of Paul that we read in our morning lesson. Paul is so audacious as to state that he is the incarnation of certain constructive values that he wants his friends to make a part of their lives. Constructive values have life only as someone becomes an incarnation of such values.

- The only useful definition of love is in the life of some loving person.
- Justice has reality only as I experience justice at the hands of a just person.
- Honesty takes shape when someone deals with me honestly.

You can write elaborate definitions of any value. You can even write a book on the subject of constructive values; however, it is only as certain people become the incarnation of those values that something good happens in our lives and in the world. So Paul is not being audacious when he suggests that his friends copy his example; there is nothing else which we can copy in life but living examples of goodness. In two references in the I Corinthians (4: 16 and 11: 1), Paul says to his friends, "...be imitators of me." This does not mean that Paul's churches were personality cults in which Paul, his cause, and his theology were lionized. What it means is that Paul recognized that, whether we know it or not, there is an inescapable interaction of human personalities and that people do influence one another.

Let me make the important distinction that character is not to be confused with anything else that people leave in the world. There are things that people leave behind them that we must never confuse with character. After people have departed this world, we may be left with their property, their money, their business, their program, their cause, their system of belief, or the ideology that they espoused. Sometimes we will watch their children, heirs, or followers attempting to carry on for them, keeping the family business intact, sitting at Dad's desk and lunching at Dad's club, or keeping Dad's cause and ideology alive in the world. These are all futile and substitute devices for keeping a departed cat alive. And we never can or need to keep anyone's departed soul alive. If they have given the world the enduring gift of good character, they continue to have a place in the world, even when we are not remembering them.

Do you hear what I am saying? You can't keep someone alive who has left nothing of good character in the world. Keeping their business or estate intact, carrying on their cause, or going to their grave will not give life to someone who has not already left in the world some living, loving gift of character. If the interaction of their character with yours has left some imprint of love, justice, kindness, and goodness upon your character, they already have their continuing place in the world, even if you don't keep their cause alive or make seasonal visits to their grave. Even if such a good person has no children or family to remember them, the heritage of their character has, nonetheless, made its mark upon someone and has enriched the stream of the world's ongoing life. As we pray in one of the prayers in the burial service, "...we thank you for the goodness and truth that have passed from her life into the lives of others and have made the world richer for her presence."

I will admit to being a terrible sentimentalist about animals. I cling tenaciously to the memory of all our departed pets. As silly as it seems, we still have not buried the ashes of either Winston or Churchill. However, I know that such silliness does not keep them alive. The thing that matters most to me is something that our David said on the night of Winston's death. He said simply, "No matter what happened, Winston was always there."

And now you know that I am not talking just about animals in this sermon. There are certain special people who come into our lives who love us unconditionally. They are continuing incarnations of God's unconditional love for us in Christ. No one can ever replace such lovely people; no one needs to, because they will always be there.

No cat will ever beat Morgan; but then, no cat ever needs to. He'll always have his place. He'll always be there.

The Whole Story*

September 22, 1991

Scripture Lesson: **I John 2: 7 - 3: 3.**

We discovered a delightful watering place over in central Pennsylvania this past summer. Probably some of you have been there and will recognize my description of it; however, because it might constitute a free commercial for that establishment, I shall omit the mention of its name. This is a resort inn and playhouse located just south of Carlisle in the lovely country town of Boiling Springs. It appears that a majority of the guests go there to eat, recreate, and enjoy the offerings of the playhouse.

There are, however, other justifications for stopping there: the inn happens to be situated on an old estate through which passes one of the finest trout streams in Pennsylvania, the famous Yellow Breeches. It has been so named since the time of the American Revolution when British soldiers, attempting to wash their clothes in the creek, discovered that, for some reason, the mineral content of the stream caused a yellow discoloration of their white breeches.

In one of the dining rooms of the several buildings on the property, there is a large mural which goes back to the days of the family who owned the estate before it became an inn. This particular mural depicts a country scene in which the owner, a Dr. Sadler, is hunting with his bird dogs. When one views this mural, it is not too difficult to discern the fact that something has been altered. In the original mural, Dr. Sadler was not alone; a close friend and his hunting dog were also in the picture. However, for some reason, Dr. Sadler and his friend had a furious disagreement which ended their friendship. Immediately thereafter, this former friend was painted out of the picture. Let's think about two ideas:

DON'T PAINT ANYTHING OUT OF YOUR PAST

We are a product of our whole history. Whether we are talking about the institutional history of a church or the individual history of a person, our institutional or personal health is related to our recognition and acceptance of our whole story. We are products of the many chapters of our story and of the many changes through which we have passed in those chapters. Don't ever try to pretend that a part of your past didn't happen; all of it was a necessary part of what and who you are today.

Our youngest daughter, Holly, spent some time with us in August. She brought with her a delightful young man who, early one morning over coffee, in the old-fashioned manner, asked me for permission to marry her. I told him that she was not really mine to "give" away and that if she were, I might have done so on several occasions during her teens. But I also told him that I was delighted to consent to their marriage and to welcome him into the family.

During the course of their visit, we spent a whole evening viewing all the slides that tell Holly's story from the day when we went to the adoption agency to get her, on through her terrible teens. As hard as we tried, nothing we showed him could change his mind! However, as we viewed these slides, something else was going on in my mind: I couldn't believe what I was seeing of myself. It was not just that I was almost 30 years younger in those pictures. Yes, I had more hair, and the clothing was that of the 1960's, and during much of that time, I wore a clerical collar on every day of the week. But it was something more than my outward appearance. Maybe it was the interior memory of what I was like in those days -- memories of both high ideals and terrible failures, or maybe even the lack of memories and the mystery of just who I was way back then. In summary, I had the feeling that I was viewing pictures of someone whom I had forgotten, of someone who isn't me any more, and of someone I don't have to be and don't want to be any more.

Still, I knew that person was me, and there was no denying it. The more I watched, the more I realized that, for better or worse, that was who I had to be back then. I had to pass through that chapter, fight certain battles, winning some and losing others. I had to learn certain skills and lessons, and make certain mistakes. So, I came away thankful that I was not that me any more, but realizing that it was necessary for me to be that person back then. When the lights came on and the slide show was over, I felt a bit more whole. I felt as though I had experienced a healthy reunion with a past piece of myself, that I had restored an original portion of my personal mural that, previously, I had painted out of the picture.

There was something therapeutic about that experience. Indeed, is this not what often happens in therapy, as some skilled guide helps us to go back into a forgotten or rejected past so that we experience the feelings that we did not allow ourselves to have back then? Healthy persons and healthy institutions value the lessons of their whole story. There is no health to be had in pretending that the past did not happen.

We are a church with a rich and varied history. Some elements of the past are gone and forgotten; others persist and remain until this day. The morning coats of the ushers remind us of a day of dignity and formality; in this day when "anything goes," there may be more validity than we realize in retaining them. More important than that are the memories of the different styles of ministry which we have known. For a few older members, Shadyside Church will always be the poetry of Dr. Kerr's style. For many others, it will always be the pastoral ministry of Dr. Scharfe. And for still many others, it will continue to be the clear cadence of Dr. Holland's delivery. All three of them are with us still, and all of the things that happened during their ministries have left their indelible mark on our personality.

When I went to my first little church, all I ever heard about was the devoted 26-year ministry of the Reverend Seth Craig. He was not my immediate predecessor; another preacher, Joseph Pringle, had been ground to powder in the three years before I came to that pulpit. He, too, had been continually reminded about how Mr. Craig did it. Confident that I was more durable than Mr. Pringle, I set out to assault the haunting heritage of Mr. Craig. Whenever I learned that he had done things one way, I would deliberately do them the other way. When I learned what his weaknesses were, I set out to excel in those areas. When I heard of his strengths, I pretended that those skills didn't matter. It was as though I was trying to pretend that Mr. Craig never existed; it was as though I was trying, stupidly, to paint him out of the picture.

And then one day the news came that his widow was seriously ill. She had moved to the upstate farm in northern New York where Mr. Craig had died during the first year after his retirement. I can't remember why (it may have been someone else's suggestion), but I still somehow had a half ounce of common sense which told me that I ought to go and visit her. I made the long trip from Newburgh up to Cambridge, New York, where I found her in a small hospital. Mrs. Craig was a plain, old-fashioned, country-style minister's wife. Whether or not she had heard much about me I did not know, but she told me all the wonderful things she had heard about me and how delighted she was that I was one of her dear husband's successors. Her warmth and generosity lovingly enfolded me. In her countrified way, she let me know that I was all right just the way I was, just as Mr. Craig was all right the way he was. Later that day, I met her sons, who accorded me the same warm acceptance.

My ministry at that church had its real beginning on that day. I knew I didn't have to paint out any part of the church's past. I stopped fighting Mr. Craig's memory; I even tried to do some of things that he did, although I could never do them his way. I also concentrated on doing my own thing, but now, in a quieter spirit, and without vengeance. On the Sunday before my last Sunday in that church (after my 10 years of ministry there), we celebrated the 125th anniversary. In the morning service of that day, we dedicated the new outdoor chimes which had been installed -- in memory of Mr. and Mrs. Craig.

Don't Paint Anything Out Of Your Past

And while you're at it, remember something else that's important:

LEAVE SOME ROOM IN THE MURAL OF YOUR LIFE FOR THE FUTURE YOU

We are all in the process of becoming something and someone other than we are now. "Beloved, we are God's children now; what we will be has not yet been revealed." (3: 2). If I have had to pass through many rather different chapters of my story to become the person I am today, then I must realize that the person who I am today is also someone in transition, moving on toward yet another stage.

I can hear someone saying, "Well, that's encouraging!" I can also hear someone else saying, "No, that's scary." In a sense, it's like going into surgery. You give up control of your life to these other people who put you to sleep and work on you. On the one hand, you may feel encouraged to know that, when you wake up, they will have relieved you of your problem. At other times, however, there is something exploratory about the surgery, and you won't know until you wake up what it is that had to be done to you. So, there's both encouragement and fear in the realization that our life is not totally in our control, that we are in the mysterious process of becoming something and someone other than we are today.

After all, what you have been in the past and what you are today is something of a mystery, which you cannot totally explain and for which you cannot take total credit. You and I cannot say that we have been in total control of our lives. We can't take credit for the way the changing chapters turned out.

I look at the person I was in those slides realizing that the young minister in a clerical collar with a full head of brown hair had no idea of where he was headed. He thought he did, but really he didn't. He didn't have the foggiest notion of the successes or the failures through which he would pass in the coming years. He had no notion of the sheer happiness that would simply come his way without his creating it or deserving it, nor of the heartbreaking disappointments which would also be a part of his story. He could not know of the people who were waiting in the wings to come onto the stage and into his story, nor of those who would make their exit before he was ready to let go of them. You and I would never have been able to guess what has happened to us in our journey through the stages and chapters of our lives.

So we don't know what we're becoming. We can make the best decisions we know how to make, and we know that those decisions will have some effect upon the outcome. We can also make some bad decisions, which can thwart God's best plans for us. However, we are Calvinists, children of the Reformed tradition, and we believe in the loving sovereignty of God. So, both our theology and our experience tell us that some higher power is shaping the process of our becoming. As Professor Orr of Pittsburgh Seminary used to phrase it, there is a "guided drift" to the movement of our lives. This means that we can be patient and hopeful about our lives together as God's people. We're just children, the children of God, passing through necessary stages of growth. There are things that will be changing in our individual lives, as well as in the life of our church family. As we change, the church will change. We will learn to love some of the people who, today, make it difficult for us to love them. Then too, there will be new people coming into our lives and into our church family who will play a part in what we will become as a community of faith. And all of this is in other hands; indeed, in the best and wisest of hands. Jesus Christ, the same yesterday, today, and forever, is still the great head of the church. And it is into his image and likeness that we are growing. Listen again to the promise: "Beloved, we are God's children now; what we will be has not yet been revealed. What we do know is this: when he is revealed, we will be like him, for we will see him as he is. And all who have this hope in him purify themselves, just as he is pure."

* *This sermon was preached at the beginning of Shadyside Church's 125th anniversary observance.*

$\mathscr{M}$onument from the Minority

....

November 17, 1991

Scripture Lesson: ***Exodus 23: 1-13.***

❦

COMMENTS ON THE LESSON

$\mathscr{P}$reachers are often accused of having the bad habit of returning continually to the same set of favorite Biblical texts for expressing the convictions (or prejudices, as the case may be) that are dear to their hearts. The term used by Biblical scholars for describing this favorite set of texts and passages is called the "canon within the canon." By that we mean that, within the official collection of canonical scripture which we call "the Bible," whether or not we are preachers, we all tend to have a "little Bible" composed of those special texts which, for us, best summarize the meaning of the entire Bible. If we were sentenced to exile on some desert island and could not carry our entire Bible with us, we would want to take this smaller collection of passages and texts. This would be our "Bible within the Bible," our "canon within the canon."

To relieve preachers of this habit of always "pumping" the same texts year after year, it is often recommended that preachers follow a lectionary of texts from the entire Bible so that their sermons will cover the entire range of doctrines and themes to which a congregation ought to be exposed on a regular basis. Such lectionaries are prepared by various denominations, and in certain churches (such as the Catholic and Episcopal churches), most of the preachers follow them faithfully. In other denominations, like ours, preaching from a lectionary is optional.

However, even if a lectionary is followed, there are certain passages of scripture that never make it into any lectionary and are hardly ever (or maybe never) preached upon by any preacher anywhere. I suspect that our lesson this morning is one such passage. It is typical of certain Old Testament passages that seem simply too obscure and antiquated to have much value for a New Testament congregation in the modern world.

What we are reading is a smattering of seemingly unrelated ancient Hebrew laws from the Book of Exodus. Immediately following the delivery of the Ten Commandments in the 20th chapter, there is a collection of various laws related to specific legal cases that would have arisen in the tribal life of the Hebrew people. For various technical reasons that I shall not recite, this collection is called the Covenant Code. Although their placement in the Book of Exodus leaves the first impression that they come from the time of Moses, their specific content reflects the situation of a settled agricultural community: a kind of established agrarian life that simply did not exist in the time of Moses. However, some later editors have placed them here, as though they originated in the time of Moses. But, maybe they do go back to a very early time in the sense of representing the accumulated wisdom of many centuries. The best laws always have such tried and true experience as their basis. Such laws work; they are observed because centuries of life experience have taught people that these rules make sense.

This passage may seem to be a collection of unrelated laws that have been lumped together, side by side, despite their unrelatedness. Before we are finished considering our subject today, perhaps we will see that they are, nonetheless, tied together by a common spirit of reverence and care for God's gift of life to all of his creatures.

SERMON

It was during the last weekend of October when something about this morning's lesson seized my attention. I was studying it in connection with our Kerygma Bible Study Course. In that course we have been studying the manner in which the concept of law is understood in the Hebrew and Christian scriptures. What got my attention was a new rendering of a word in the passage. You will notice that in the old RSV translation, which you have in your pew Bibles, the rendering of

Exodus 23: 2 reads, "You shall not follow a multitude to do evil...." This does not grasp our attention because "multitude" is such a frequent term in the Bible. When I hear it, I see Jesus preaching to the multitudes, or else I see the great multitude singing songs of heavenly praise, as envisioned by the Book of Revelation.

However, in the NRSV, as you may have noted when I read it, the new rendering for "multitude" is "majority." That is the real sense of the context. "You shall not follow a majority in wrongdoing ... you shall not side with the majority so as to pervert justice...." I think you can see why this caught my attention in the week before Election Day. It continued to hold my attention until the days after the election when I was arranging my thoughts in manuscript form and listening to the interestingly different ways in which the two parties interpreted the various possible meanings of the majority vote.

Our entire political system operates around the will of the majority. With various checks, balances, and modifications, a democracy operates by majority rule. We have also seen the increasing importance of predicting the opinions and feelings of the majority before an election is held. Candidates must determine what will sell with the majority of voters; to get elected, candidates must be able to guess what the people want to hear. Once elected, public officials continue their search to find how the majority of their constituents want to be led. Nowadays, we wonder whether we are being ruled by principles or by polls.

Politicians have always wanted to stay in touch with the majority in shaping their campaigns as candidates or their policies as leaders, but our modern computerized methods of determining majority opinion have given a whole new face to the idea of majority rule. Although the will of the majority is at the heart of democracy, politics by polls has raised a whole new set of issues for Western democracy. We find ourselves asking whether majorities are always right. Does public opinion, formed by all kinds of forces, inform us with accuracy about what is best for the public? Isn't there a place for courageous leadership with informed principle? But can such informed, principled persons get elected?

It is interesting that the Bible, which we view as having had such a powerful influence in the history of Western democracy, is somehow suspicious of majorities. It is a product of and advocate for the minority. The passage before us comes at this matter in such a radical manner.

In the opening paragraph, we are reminded that, in matters of litigation, the opinion of the majority may be all wrong. The tendency of humans to "run with the herd" teaches us that hanging parties seldom act justly and that majorities can become mobs. For that matter, with all of the Bible's concern for the poor, this opening paragraph reminds us that even a mob of poor people can be wrong in their judgment. This is interesting material. We want to read more about this idea; however, the passage takes a strange turn.

It turns to the subject of my enemy's ox or donkey. "When you come upon your enemy's ox or donkey going astray, you shall bring it back. When you see the donkey of one who hates you lying under its burden and you would hold back from setting it free, you must help to set it free." If you humans can't get along with one another, for God's sake, don't take it out on the poor, speechless animals! God is concerned with the utter minority fringe: the poor beasts who have no voice to speak for their own minority rights.

Understandably, the passage moves on to speak on behalf of the poor. The context again is the lawsuit, and evidently, the poor have always had a hard time in court -- back then as well as nowadays. The real measure of justice in a society is how well the legal system works for the poor who can't afford fancy lawyers. For example, as we form our opinions about capital punishment, we need to remember that electric chairs and gas chambers are built almost entirely for poor people. The sons and daughters of fine families are seldom executed; they have a voice in court that the poor seldom have. The same goes for resident aliens, whose concerns are mentioned next; they, too, must not be oppressed simply because there aren't many of them.

And then, in another radical turn, God's concern is expressed for the land: give it a rest in the seventh year. Let the poor gather its fruits in that year, and -- listen to this --what the poor don't take, leave that for the wild animals.

Finally, remember to do no work on the sabbath. Why? Not for the reasons given in the Ten Commandments (relating it to God's rest), but so that your ox and donkey, slave and alien -- in that order -- may have rest!

I read that we're going to have a new radio talk show which will be making fun of animal rights advocates. Well, the Bible doesn't view the careless treatment of animals as a laughing matter. In fact, it seems to suggest that the acid test of a just society may be found in an area where we least suspect: in our concern for the most voiceless of all minorities, the so-called dumb beasts.

Well, of course, there's another side to this whole matter in the Bible. We have to admit that there's an awful lot of killing in the Bible. Although in some ways, the Bible is far ahead of the barbaric times in which it arose, it is in other ways very much a part of those times. There are lots of bloody sacrifices and lots of bloody battles in which God's people kill the native people of the land of Canaan (not wholly unlike the way in which we took land and life from Native Americans). And, obviously too, vegetarianism was not the rule of life in Israel, although probably no people in history have had the thing about meat that people seem to have in our society.

Still, even in some of its seeming complicity with ancient barbaric ways, the Bible rises above its times and displays fine truths, which are like shafts of light breaking through and into a thick jungle of filth and imbecility. "An eye for an eye, a tooth for a tooth," the law of revenge *(lex talionis),* seems primitive to us, but it offered a cap for bringing to an end those tribal blood feuds which went on for generations. Here was a formula for quick and final satisfaction of the demands of justice.

Even if, in some ways, we get a mixed signal from the Bible, it is still, in other ways, far ahead of our own time. If, in Israel, people killed for food, they never made a sport out of killing for fun. If people were stoned to death for specific crimes, the Bible nonetheless distinguishes carefully between killing for self-defense and murderous deeds inspired by hatred or vengeance. What is even more, the Hebrew scriptures recognized the slow death that takes place in a society in which there are endless spirals of poverty and affluence, and in which the poor get poorer while the rich get richer. In its law for the year of Jubilee, Hebrew scripture ended those cycles by calling for a return of all ancestral property every fifty years. Everyone would go back to "go" and start all over again in that year and earn their own way, without the advantage or disadvantage of their old man's fortune or bad luck.

"You shall not follow a majority in wrongdoing...." In God's kingdom, might does not make right, whether it is the might of numbers or the might of money or the might of being born into the right tribe (our crowd, our kind, our pure race). In the kingdom of God, we are called to live in right relatedness with all of God's creatures and with all of God's creation. We are to obey his law of love and justice, even if no one is doing it, even if obedience enjoys only a minimal return.

Last summer, I read two articles which appeared following the death of Isaac Bashevis Singer. I am wondering how many Christians have read his stories. I wonder that because he wrote in a language that so few people understand: Yiddish. I suppose not too many, that is, until he became popular by winning the Nobel Prize in Literature in 1978. Before that, one supposes that his principal audience was Jewish, because much of his early material was confined to those who could read the Yiddish-language newspaper, *(The Daily Forward)*, a New York publication in which his stories began appearing in 1935. When he won the Nobel Prize, he became the first recipient in the history of the Swedish Academy to begin his acceptance lecture in Yiddish. My guess is that, following this recognition, his readership increased. Maybe it also increased after one of his stories was made into a Barbra Streisand movie entitled *Yentl,* from his short story of similar title, *Yentl the Yeshiva Boy.*

Many of his stories are about Eastern European Jews living in the old country, but also about their ancestors living in America. His stories are permeated by his Hebrew faith, but they are not religious in the usual sense. He does not tell us how much comfort one can derive from one's faith amidst the tribulations of life, but instead, about how much pain one must endure with good humor despite one's faith. His faith is a running argument with God; while he cannot conceive of life without faith in God, he keeps complaining to God about all the promises that God never seems to keep. In particular, he writes with painful beauty about old Jewish widows and widowers who cling to some thread of faith in the barren loneliness of their final days.

What interested me were some comments made to a reviewer about what Singer felt to be the final significance of his life. He had decided early in life to become a devoted vegetarian. With typical dry humor, he told of how this delivered him from the hazard of having his wife place a greasy bowl of chicken soup on one of his manuscripts. But it also became a commitment through which he could make a statement about his central faith. His reviewer wrote:

"From childhood on he had seen that might makes right, that man is stronger than chicken -- man eats chicken, not vice versa. That bothered him, for there was no evidence that people were more important than chickens. About this decision, he commented, 'So, in a very small way, I do a favor for the chickens.... If I will ever get a monument, chickens will do it for me'."

I hope that my life leaves some monument of protest against the idea that majorities are the measure of justice, that might makes right, and that I need a pollster to help me form my moral and ethical principles. I also hope that some of God's voiceless people and creatures, even if they can't build me a monument, are glad that I lived and that I spoke for them, even if what I said and did didn't help. I'd like to come to the end and have someone say, "Thanks for trying." That, it seems to me, is why we humans are here: not to succeed, because unfailing success is only for the gods, but instead, as fallible humans whom God has graciously loved and accepted, at least to try.

The Power to Bless

March 15, 1992

Scripture Lessons: **Genesis 25: 27-34 and 27
(Selections), Romans 12: 14-21.**

Before an official call can be extended to a pastor by a Presbyterian church, the prospective candidate must first be examined and approved by Presbytery's Committee on Ministry. Back when Dr. Harold Scott was our Presbytery Executive, after the committee had completed the required oral examination, Dr. Scott would unofficially and humorously induct the incoming minister into what he called "The Order of the Calloused Thumb." It was Dr. Scott's way of reminding incoming pastors of the importance of the old-fashioned pastoral work of making hospital and house calls as a way of keeping in touch with their members. He used to conclude his remarks with the reminder that "the minister who is invisible throughout the week will probably be incomprehensible on Sunday." He was reminding us that effective preaching needs something more than many hours spent in the seclusion of our study; it also needs to be nourished by contact with our people. Granted, we must spend considerable time with our books, especially in the careful exegesis of scripture; but our sermons must also grow out of our common life with all kinds of people.

And that's how this sermon had its beginnings. I had just parked in the parking lot of one of our local hospitals. At the end of the lot closest to the hospital, there was a row of spaces reserved for the handicapped. Only one car was parked in those designated parking places, and that is probably why I noticed what was happening. The driver of that one car was the handicapped person, and he was struggling to get a collapsible wheelchair out of the back seat of his two-door car. With a two-door car, that's a challenging task, even for a person who is not handicapped. Somehow or other, the wheelchair appeared to be stuck on some object, and so I asked him if I could lend a hand. When he indicated that such help might be appreciated, I dislodged the wheel chair and opened it for him.

I realize that we can be overly solicitous in offering aid to handicapped persons; they can do many more things than we realize, and it can be insulting to infer that they must be helped with every detail. When he seemed to infer that he could manage the rest of the job, I left the task of getting into the wheelchair to him; but as I took my leave, he looked up at me cheerfully and said, "God bless you!"

His word of blessing, for some reason, made me feel good. Perhaps that's why, as I walked toward the hospital, I mentioned to the security guard in the driveway that he might want to keep his eye on the man getting out of the two-door car, just in case he might need any further assistance.

About ten minutes later, after I had checked the hospital clergy list, I headed back to the parking lot, still feeling good about having been blessed, until I noticed that the handicapped man had just then finally managed to get himself into the wheelchair. He had been struggling for a full ten minutes, and the security guard had simply stood by, doing nothing to help. So now, I found myself with a curious set of feelings.

I was feeling good for having been blessed by the man in the wheelchair, but I was also feeling self-righteous about my having done something to help. Then, too, I was also feeling angry at the security guard for his indifference and generally annoyed at the sort of people who are indifferent to the rights and needs of handicapped persons. And I was feeling particularly incensed at the ones who, in addition to their general indifference, park their cars in spaces that are reserved for the handicapped. Having been blessed only a few minutes before, I had allowed my emotions to reach such a state that I was close to calling down a curse upon all such callous souls.

There is a very thin wall between our power to bless and our power to curse. I remembered the words of James: "From the same mouth comes blessing and cursing. My brothers and sisters, this ought not to be so." (James 3: 10).

For the rest of that day, however, I thought more about what really is meant when someone says to us, "God bless you," and why it can engender good feelings. Is it nothing more than a mix of various egotistic emotions in which self-righteousness, self-justification, and self-esteem get mixed together in a pleasant-tasting, high-producing brew? Or is there something of deeper significance? Let's try on this idea:

We need to cultivate a renewed respect for the mysterious reality that lies beneath our power to both bless and curse one another.

I use the term "mysterious reality" to describe something that, although we may not be able to explain it, has a real existence that we cannot doubt.

I cannot explain this amazing power that we have -- a power that can pass even between total strangers, mind you! -- unless I work upon the assumption that there are deep connections between all human beings. I am saying that God has built connections into our created being, that we are not made to stand alone, and that we were made for life with one another, just as much as we were made to live in relationship with God. You have often heard me say that there is an empty place at the center of our souls that can be filled only by God; I am adding to that that there is something about our soul stuff that needs positive relationships with all kinds of people. Only the most spiritually advanced souls could dare to live as hermits, and even the most saintly hermits needed to come together from time to time.

When we bless one another, we are sending energy across the lines of these invisible connections, using them in the way they were meant to be used, with the result that we feel healed and whole. But when we curse one another, we are sending a destructive energy across them which actually hurts us, both the one who curses and the one who is cursed.

A year or so ago, I had a furious altercation with a florist who was interfering with our wedding procedures. In previous weddings, he had been abusive and discourteous to our volunteer wedding coordinators and to our secretarial staff and had been told not to enter our building again until he was willing to apologize and be cooperative. When I reminded him of this and instructed him to remove himself from the building, he resorted again to his verbal abuse. I remained firm and didn't retreat one inch! (I realize that I may often seem to be like Clark Kent, mild-mannered reporter of the Daily Planet, but when attacked, I can be as formidable as Mighty Mouse!)

Knowing that I would not back down, he stomped out of the narthex and, in loud tones, declared me to be a "miserable old (something I cannot say in the pulpit)." I tried to cover my own disturbance at being thus cursed by treating it humorously and saying to those about me that what he said was only partly true. I am not miserable about being what I am; instead, I am a "happy old (something I cannot say in the pulpit)." Still, I know, and you know too, that when we experience such a furious altercation, it hurts our system. Had there been a lab technician present, it could have been demonstrated that this curse had resulted in an increase in my blood pressure and heart rate. Curses are harmful and hurtful, and to some extent, their effect can be physically measured.

Indeed, probably the best proof of the mysterious reality of our power to bless comes from the opposite direction: we have all experienced the reality of our power to curse. Although we cannot always measure and demonstrate the positive results of being blessed, we have seen what happens to persons who live continually in the presence of cursing.

We have seen it particularly with children. A child who is cursed at becomes accursed, and the effects are usually lifelong. When, with rage and anger, a child is told by a parent to "get the hell out of the way," the message is effective and lifelong in its power. The child will learn, on into adulthood, to stay on the sidelines of life and to have little confidence in his or her worth and abilities. If you take time to think through all of the common curse words, you will begin to discover that all of them, quite literally, shape the way in which we think about ourselves, about persons of the opposite sex, and about the world and God.

For that matter, if you take time to reflect upon it, you may have very distinct and visual memories of those occasions when your parents swore at you. As an adult, you may have related them to others in a joking manner, but what is significant is how precisely you remember the exact scenery and details of the moment you were cursed.

And let's remember too that children can be cursed without our ever using any curse word. With perfect propriety, and within a setting of affluence and culture, a child can be verbally abandoned and told to "get the hell out of the way." And that fear of abandonment -- with the accompanying inability to trust even those who love us for fear of losing them -- the fear of being left on the sidelines of life can be permanent.

Our power to curse knows no boundaries of class, culture, education, or income. In any home or setting, there are lapses of love that are fatal: hateful words that can never be unsaid and hurtful actions that cannot be undone. When we consider the irrevocable realities of our human interrelatedness, we do well, as did old Isaac, to tremble violently.

However, while we cannot always measure it, we remember what health and wholeness follow the lives of those who are touched with blessing. Be sure to read again the story of how Jesus blessed and touched children (Mark 10: 13-16). It is interesting that the children brought to him on that day were not afflicted with illness. Their parents wanted Jesus to touch them. And we read that he did exactly that: "he took them up in his arms (obviously, they were little and could not understand what was happening), laid his hands on them, and blessed them." (Wouldn't you like to read a novel or short story about one of these children and of how, as they grew up, and all through their life, they lived with the curious sense of being surrounded by a loving and friendly presence?)

Maybe we need to recapture some of the ancient respect and superstitious reverence for the power of language that we find in the Bible. There are little words and actions that have healing power.

Take the words, "Thank you!" Actually, they constitute a prayer of thanksgiving addressed to another human being. They express the sentiment, "Thanks be to you!" When said with sincerity and meaning, they acknowledge our inescapable interdependence and interrelatedness with the entire human family. Unfortunately, we often teach our children to say "thank you" as a matter of mere politeness or correctness. When taken and said seriously, saying "thank you" acknowledges the fact that none of us can make it on our own; we need all sorts of common, and even lowly people, for our mere survival. If you doubt that, try drawing your own water; try raising, processing, and preserving your own food, without the benefit of an electric range and refrigerator; or try living without garbage collection for three weeks! We all depend absolutely upon one another and are seriously and totally interconnected.

One of the most saintly souls I have ever known, in the last hours of her life, with little breath left in her, gasped out the words "thank you," because I moistened her lips with water. Even at the very end, when she could have abandoned all the usual polite courtesies, she acknowledged her ties with the human family. And maybe that constant awareness of the ties that bind us all together, and the desire to use those ties for blessing -- maybe that was the simple source of her saintliness.

But let me tell you, in closing, how that day ended, that day upon which a disabled man blessed me. On my way home, at about 8:00 p.m., I stopped at the Forbes Gerontology Center to visit one of our members. She is an elderly lady who, as the result of a stroke, has suffered an impairment of her speech. So, I leaned over the side of the bed rail, kept my face close to hers, and spoke slowly to her, holding her hand and offering a brief prayer. At the end of the prayer, she let go of my hand and, with her hand, patted the side of my face, and whispered, "Good boy!"

Well, I'm not a good boy; I have often been a very bad boy. For that matter, I often feel that I'm a bad boy even when I have been a good boy. So I need the assurance of pardon at the beginning of our worship service; I need it as much, and maybe even more, than the rest of you, because I really need to feel forgiven before I stand up and try to speak the word of God to you. I need not only that assurance, but also the word of acceptance, which tells me that, because of God's grace, I am accepted -- if not good, at least, acceptable.

And that is what that dear lady's little touch and whispered blessing conveyed to me: assurance of God's gracious acceptance of me. Because of the grace of God, manifested in Jesus Christ, I am accepted, just as I am. And you are accepted, just as you are.

You may carry with you the unhealed hurts and open wounds of many cursings that life has laid upon you, but God is always ready to bless you with his loving acceptance. I did not say "ready and waiting," because he does not wait; sometimes, he conveys his blessing through strangers and dear old sick souls who are at the edge of life. And sometimes, if we will, he can use our little words and touches to convey the blessing of his grace.

The power that we possess is awesome in the good that it can accomplish. So, as Paul commands, "... bless and do not curse.... Rejoice with those who rejoice, weep with those who weep.... Live in harmony with one another; do not be haughty, but associate with the lowly ... if your enemies are hungry, feed them; if they are thirsty, give them something to drink.... Do not be overcome by evil, but overcome evil with good."

And finally, may God bless you!

𝒮inging Pastors and Prophets*

October 25, 1992

❧

ℬecause today's service represents our recognition of, and commitment to a ministry of music in our church, the decision was made to follow something of the old traditional format of a service of installation for a pastor, in which there would be delivered a charge to the pastor, followed by a second charge to the congregation. And so, my words are for Dr. Walker, but also for the members of his music staff and choir. I speak to those to whom we have committed the leadership of our music ministry; the rest of you are invited to listen in on what I want to say to them.

I started reading an interesting book last summer. Although it has almost no connection with the subject of music, I found it to be saying some things that speak significantly to what we are about this morning. It was a book by a physician (and also a first-class writer) who reflects upon his life as a doctor, as well as upon his upbringing as the son of a doctor.

If you're wondering why I would possibly even think of reading such a book, then let me tell you that I was drawn to it by its title: *Down From Troy, A Doctor Comes Of Age.* What seized my imagination was that the author and I were born in the same year, 1928, and in the same city, Troy, New York, and that his father probably practiced at the hospital where I was born. The author is Dr. Richard Selzer, a retired professor of surgery at the Yale Medical School.

I cannot and need not take time to tell you all of the interesting memories that this book evoked, and how it confirmed some suspicions that I had always harbored about the place of my birth. Richard Selzer was brought up in the better end of town, and he lived in Troy all through his growing up. That was not the case with me; my family moved to nearby Schenectady. Still, his story was rich with associations.

What spoke to me for our purposes this morning was his larger artistic and holistic view of what a hospital is meant to be as a therapeutic community and temple of healing (those are my words, not his).

Because he himself was a doctor, he could be critical of his own profession and of the acutely exalted sense of self-importance that, in his view, plagues many members of the medical profession. He was critical of the bearing of omnipotence with which doctors would often enter a ward, of how some of them seemed to believe that some "disembodied radiance" of their healing presence lingered on, even after they had made their exit. His description of such doctors in their relationship to the hospital's healing mission could be applied to the same exaggerated sense of self-importance that some of us pastors display in our relationship to the church and its healing mission.

His main point was that a lot of healing goes on in a hospital quite apart from the specific work of the doctors. For example, while he himself does not profess to be a person of religious faith, he extolled the healing ministry of the devoted nuns who nursed at St. Mary's Hospital in Troy. He remembers how those quiet sisters were gathered around his father's bed as he lay dying (his father was Jewish) and how their faces were like lamps in the darkness, "glowing with an imperturbable golden light."

He speaks a good word also for the old-fashioned, large 30-bed wards, which used to be provided for the less affluent patients in the hospitals of yesteryear. He feels not only that they were safer than the private rooms in which a patient is out of sight to the nursing staff, but also that they provided a dimension of therapy often unnoticed. Patients could commiserate with one another.

However, beyond recognizing these other participants in the healing process, the nurses and the patients themselves, Dr. Selzer is interested in the artistry with which an architect designs a hospital. He calls attention to an unnoticed healing factor in the manner in which bricks, wood, steel, and glass can be so employed as to make a hospital a true temple of human wholeness. He asks that architects design buildings that will be infused with sunlight, because the light of the sun is necessary for the deep healing of the human spirit. He dreams of a hospital so situated that every patient can enjoy the sunset. And he further believes that every hospital should have a large reflecting pool and high-rising fountain. Water is healing and cleansing, and falling water can teach us how to comply with our weakness by surrendering to "peaceful horizontality."

As I read these things about all of the elements that play a vital part in the healing mission of a hospital, I was hearing some things that we preachers need to hear and consider:

There's a lot of ministry that goes on in a church quite apart from, and in addition to, the ministry of the ministers.

There's a lot of preaching that goes on in a church quite apart from, and in addition to, the preaching of the preachers.

I could actually direct this thought to you, the members of the congregation, because there are ways in which you carry on the ministry of this church. Indeed, sometimes you can provide a more effective pastoral ministry to certain members of the church than can we who are ordained. And, there are ways in which you are the major sermon that this church is proclaiming to the world. If they don't hear and see the truth of the gospel in your daily life, my weekly words are somehow robbed of their power.

This morning, however, I want to say to John Walker and our choir that, as you perform your ministry of music, I charge you to remember that the ministry of church music is both a pastoral and a prophetic ministry.

There are some things that church music is not:

- It is not background music to help set the mood for what the ministers are saying.
- It is not provided as a musical interlude to fill the vacuum -- to provide a break between the speaking parts of the service or some thing to fill the empty silence when the talking stops.

• It is not elevator music to fill our minds as we ascend to the top floor, to the sermonic high point of the service.

There are some very large and popular churches where church music is being prostituted in this manner. It is being made into the kind of "easy listening" slush that will set the mood for a similar variety of "easy listening" sermonic slop, which poses as the preaching of the gospel. That is not our tradition in Shadyside Church. Anyone who wants that kind of fluff, froth, and feathers need not waste time waiting for it here. We mean to be a citadel of the great traditions of church music.

And that means that our music is serious in its purposes. Our intention is that our church music will be truly pastoral in its healing proclamation of the love of God and that it will be truly prophetic in its fearless proclamation of the justice of God.

Many of us have experienced the healing power of music. We have come to worship with hurting hearts, hoping to hear some hopeful word from the pulpit, which would become for us a "balm from Gilead." Sadly, however, on that Sunday, it may have been that the preacher let us down. The saving, healing word was not delivered. However, the ministry of music didn't fail us on that day. Perhaps it was a hymn or an anthem, or maybe it was the sonorous majesty of the organ. Some song did what the sermon failed to do.

However, don't ever forget that the ministry of music can also be a prophetic ministry, which cries out against injustice and oppression, challenging the hearts of those who hear. This singing ministry often does it more effectively than the word from the pulpit. How very often, in those churches where the pulpit has been silent on urgent issues of social justice, some hymn has reminded us of God's care for the poor and of those "easy speeches which comfort cruel men." The role of the singing prophet is to sing the song of justice and to raise the melodious cry of freedom. There are such hymns and anthems in abundance. We may forget many of the scorching speeches that were made during the civil rights era, but we won't forget the songs of freedom that fueled that movement.

It is no accident -- and you can observe this just by opening your Bible -- that the prophets uttered their prophecies and calls for justice in poetic form. Likewise, it is no accident that the tyrants and dictators have always feared the musicians, poets, and artists more than all their other opponents. You can always detect the first signs of a totalitarian takeover: demagogues reveal their hand by going after the artists as their early target.

You see, we can never control what may happen to people when we reach their hearts with beauty and song. When we can make the hearts of people sing; when we can show them the bright colors of God's glory; when they are liberated by beauty, they will reject the ugliness of injustice and oppression.

Don't ever think for a moment that the ministry of music is a neutral, non-controversial element of the church program. It can be the most wonderfully subversive, explosive, and dangerous ministry in which the church engages!

At Dr. Walker's urging, we have added some words of prophetic song to our weekly worship service. At the end of every sermon, we sing the closing lines of Harry Emerson Fosdick's grand hymn, *God Of Grace And God Of Glory:*

> *"Grant us wisdom, grant us courage,*
> *for the living of these days..."*

I first heard those words at the time of my graduation from Colgate University in 1950, when the speaker of the day was Dr. Fosdick. I heard them again 30 years later when I was invited back to preach the baccalaureate sermon. They remind us of how the music of praise is not only comforting, but also challenging. So, I charge you, John Walker, to challenge us by your ministry of music in our midst.

To do this, it will be necessary for you, like the prophets, to dream dreams -- dreams of love and justice for God's people. In the book that I mentioned at the beginning of this charge, Richard Selzer says of the role of artists and architects in the design of hospitals: "To create, it is necessary to dream; the artist who cannot imagine cannot prophesy."

So dream and imagine all that you can do as a singing pastor and prophet of God. In the darkest night, sing us songs that will heal our broken and lonely hearts. At the break of every Lord's day, sing for us the challenge of God's love and justice.

Sing, John Walker! Sing, you his choristers! For it is the God of the psalmists and of the prophets who is singing his song from out of the very depths of your hearts!

GOD OF THE PSALMISTS
Tune: Toulon

Dedicated to Dr. John Walker

Tune: Toulon (God of the Prophets)
10.10.10.10.

God of the psalmists! Hear this song we raise,
As in this temple your great name we praise.
In ages past, your glory filled this place;
Now in our day, reveal again your face.

Bless this your servant, called to lead our song.
Give him great faith, and spirit ever strong.
Fill him with hope that sings in darkest night;
Grant him the love that sheds abroad your light.

Give him the mind of Christ, and ears to hear
Glad songs you sing through us in each new year.
Direct his feet to follow where you will;
Strengthen his hands, his eyes with vision fill.

Send forth your people in this world's dark hour,
Raising your song of justice and of power.
Till from the heavens comes your promised sign,
And earth shall know your kingdom's grand design.

F. Morgan Roberts, 1992

* *This short sermon was a charge delivered to Dr. John Walker upon the occasion of his installation as Director of Music and Organist of Shadyside Church. The concluding hymn, God of the Psalmists, was written for that occasion by Dr. Roberts.*

The Language of Prayer

January 24, 1993

*Scripture Lesson: **Acts 10 (Selections)**.*

Early in the summer of 1954, after reading C. S. Lewis' novel *Perelandra*, the second book in his space fiction trilogy in which he made a brief and unexplained reference to the devotional life, I wrote to Professor Lewis, asking him for an explanation of his views on the prayer life. I had read somewhere that he somehow found time to answer all letters, no matter how inane they might be; and so I thought it might be worth a try to receive a response from this popular Christian author who was then coming to be regarded as the most popular apologist for the Christian faith in the English-speaking world. Before the summer had ended, I received a small, hand-addressed envelope from Magdalen College, Oxford. In it there was a one-page reply to my question. As you might gather, that letter is one of my most prized possessions. I keep it framed, and it hangs on the wall in my study here in Shadyside Church. In the event of a fire, this would be the first item I would take before evacuating the building, not only because of its sentimental value to me, but also because of its literary value as one of the letters that was included in his published correspondence.

In that letter, there was one suggestion about saying our prayers that I have never fully understood and have never regularly practiced. Lewis told me that, unless he was not feeling well or otherwise up to par, it was his practice to pray silently, without words. For some reason, I have never attempted to copy his practice; however, there was one experience many years later that got me thinking about the language of our prayers.

In previous sermons, I have mentioned how we took into our

home a young, deaf man who was having a hard time finding housing. While getting his finances in order, he lived with us for three years. On a few occasions, Jerry came to church with our David. Our service was not signed for the hearing impaired, and Jerry was totally deaf. Furthermore, he could not read lips, so there was nothing in the service that he could enjoy; the prayers, songs, and sermon had no meaning for him. After his first visit to a church service, in which I had made some humorous remark, Jerry asked our David "What were they laughing at?" He had been brought up in a severely humorless Catholic parish, and the sight of people laughing in church was new to him.

His reaction prompted a speculative question in my mind: What if God is deaf? What if we were to discover that God cannot hear all of the words that we speak and sing in worship? It is not an entirely new question; some of the Psalmists wondered why God didn't seem to hear their cries for help. How shall we speak to a God who is deaf? Contemplating that question helped me to ask some new questions about the language of our prayers. Let's work on them.

DO YOU SPEAK THE UNIVERSAL LANGUAGE OF PRAYER?

Much has changed in my lifetime in the language of prayer. I can remember when one would hear many simple, decent Christian people say, "I really can't pray in public, although I wish I could pray like Mrs. Perfect Christian does; her prayers are beautiful!" What was meant by this is that Mrs. Perfect Christian was schooled in offering prayers with the proper use of "Thee's" and "Thou's." For some reason, this was supposed to prove that Mrs. Perfect Christian could really pray -- that God really heard her prayers. Other common Christians were left feeling that their prayers were unworthy of public utterance, so they did their praying in privacy, offering simple prayers that were probably more pleasing to God than the proper prayers of Mrs. Perfect Christian.

Somewhere in the 1960's, we moved away from the formality of the King's English and the beautiful prayers of Mrs. Perfect

Christian; prayer now became contemporary and conversational. In down-to-earth terms, we talked with God about all our doubts and wonderings and used all kinds of non-liturgical language in addressing a God who no longer read Shakespeare. Then, shortly thereafter, when we began to be aware of the manner in which our traditional prayer language had always been insensitive to, and exclusive of, the spirituality of women. The language of prayer now became inclusive.

I do not want to make light of these changes in the language of prayer. If those of us who are older were programmed in the language of the King James Version, it is comforting to know that God can still understand Elizabethan English. However, those who pray fluently in fine language must realize that God can hear the prayers of the simplest souls, even the unspoken prayers of those who cannot speak at all. It is particularly important that all of us respect those who can pray fluently with inclusive language; they are keeping us aware of the biblical truth that God's nature is beyond our limited classifications of gender.

Let us learn to respect the different languages in which people of different ages and social backgrounds say their prayers, being glad for any and all sincere souls who pray. Beyond the kind of "God-language" that we use, however, we must all learn the universal language of prayer. And we will never understand that universal language until we realize that our life, far more than our words, is the most eloquent language of prayer.

Did you notice something striking in the words of God's angel to Cornelius? The angel says (10: 4), "Your prayers and your alms have ascended as a memorial before God." Throughout the Gospel of Luke and the Book of Acts, the proper attitude toward and use of our possessions is the definition of our relationship with God. Your prayers are not so much the words with which you speak to God -- whether formal, informal, or inclusive -- but rather your life and the entire sense of stewardship with which you invest yourself in God's kingdom of love and justice. The stewardship of your common, daily life is your prayer. What you do with your money, your abilities, and your time -- the significance or superficiality of it -- that is your prayer. The best book to read if you want to improve the spiritual quality of your prayers is your checkbook. Read it carefully, and it will reveal the deepest desires of your heart. It will tell you what your life is saying to God.

Many of our prayers are unanswered, because, despite the word language of our prayers, our lives are telling God what we really want -- and God is giving us exactly what we want. Our lives and our world are filled with confusion, because the selfish steward-ship of our lives is asking for and creating a confused world. Pray for peace until you're hoarse, but remember that a life of material indulgence lavished upon the triviality and tinsel of the American consumer's dream can produce nothing other than a world of hunger, poverty, and war. The universal language of prayer is a simple and sacrificial life, a life that is invested in God's kingdom of love and justice. Let's work on a second question.

ARE YOU AWARE OF THE MANY LANGUAGES OF PRAYER?

In my late teenage years, as I have previously mentioned, I was deeply involved with a very fundamentalist church. It was a church in which there was a lot of praying. Not only was there a Wednesday mid-week prayer service, there were prayer meetings of all kinds going on throughout the week. Besides the adult prayer groups, there was a prayer meeting for teenagers before the Sunday youth group meeting and another one before the Wednesday after-school Bible study group. For those of us who went to the jail service to preach to the prisoners, there was still another prayer meeting before that service.

Back in those days, I was taught to believe that having such extra prayer services was the proof that our church was a real church -- a church of true believers. It was the idea that prayer is a form of our witness to the world -- that when people would see us praying, they would know that we were the real item, the real Christians. Because of that, it was also drummed into us that one of the best ways to create an opening for telling the unsaved about our faith was by praying publicly before our meals in restaurants. The strategy was that when sinners saw us praying over our meal in a public place, they would know that we were serious about our faith. They might ask us why we did what we did, and we would tell them that we had been saved, then proceed to tell them how they could be saved. Would you believe it? I prayed over every one of my meals in the Student Union all through my college years!

Some of our high school group were so committed to such witnessing prayer that they would even pray over a chocolate sundae at the ice cream parlor where we often gathered after the Sunday evening service. Personally, I took a dim view of such hyper-devotion. It seemed to me that the prayers said over the dinner meal earlier in the evening would be sufficient to cover a late night snack!

For some reason or other, it had not occurred to those zealous souls, who used prayer as a vehicle of public witness, that the saying of prayers is not a distinctive Christian practice. All kinds of people around the world engage in the practice of prayer, both publicly and in private. Christians don't own -- nor did they invent -- the practice of prayer. For that matter, it may well be that most of the prayers addressed to the Almighty are not offered by Christians. All kinds of people of all kinds of faith say their prayers, and there are probably more of them than of us!

However, we would not have listened to such an argument, because we were actually taught that God hears only the prayers of true born-again Christians and that all other prayers, including those of Catholics and other nominal unsaved Protestants, go unheard. That might sound incredible, but that's what we were actually taught to believe. Before you call it ridiculous, let's think about it, because many of us seem to think that we are the only people who pray and that our prayers are more special to God than the prayers of the rest of the world.

Just consider the language of Christian prayers. Most of the Christian prayers that arise continually before God are not offered in the English language. I'm not a student of world population, but I would guess that Spanish is one of the languages most often heard in heaven. Even if my guess is not correct, we need to remember that English-speaking Christians do not constitute the majority of the world's Christian population. The church of Jesus Christ is growing far faster in the Third World than in the English-speaking world where, if anything, it appears to be in decline. And then there is, of course, the fact that many other people who are not Christians also pray. And some of them take their prayers more seriously than we do.

A former associate pastor of our church, Tim Solomon, is engaged in doctoral studies in the area of Christian/Muslim relations. A part of his thesis project has involved bringing together representatives of both faiths for dialogue. The Christian students participated with less than casual commitment; the Muslim students not only did their homework, but also met together to pray that they would be faithful in representing their faith. Somehow or other, we assume that we are on more intimate terms with God than those who, by reason of birth or faith, believe differently than we. How very often such is not the case. Many non-Christians go about their prayers with a devotion that shames the easygoing faith of modern American Christians.

So, we should be sympathetic with Peter, who found it difficult to believe that the world was not made up of those who were clean and unclean, just as his dietary laws had taught him the distinction between kosher and non-kosher foods. For Peter, it had been a good guys-bad guys world. How could he have suspected that, in a far away city, a Roman army officer in the enemy camp was offering prayers to God and giving alms to the poor, and that this Roman centurion's devotion was acceptable and pleasing to God. We seem unable to imagine that our faraway enemies may be offering the very same prayers and petitions before God that we ourselves are raising in the divine presence.

Did it ever occur to you what our prayers may be saying, for example, in a time of war? Our leaders, in such a time, will urge us to pray for the victory of our just cause and for the safety of our troops. Of course, the leaders in the enemy camp will be urging their people to offer the same prayers for the victory of their just cause and for the safety of their troops. (Try to picture this, for example, in the instance of the American Civil War!) However, when we pray that our battles will result in both victory and safety, we are actually praying that harm will befall the troops of the enemy. How else will victory be achieved, if it is not by the wounding and killing of the enemy? It somehow evades the scope of our prayers to realize that the families of enemy soldiers are praying for the safety of their troops, that their prayers are filled with the same thoughts and memories of their dear ones as are ours.

Whenever we say good-bye to our adult sons and daughters as they travel to some far-off land, we often see in them some mannerism or way of speaking that reminds us of the times when they were little. And if they go off to some field of battle, such memories are even more vivid and fill our minds so that we pray for them as though they were still our dear little children. Do we actually think that we are unique in such prayerful love for our children? Are the hearts of parents in an enemy land somehow devoid of those tender emotions of love that fill our hearts? Are we the only people under heaven who pray fervently and faithfully for the welfare and safety of our children?

If we were to consider the fact that our enemies pray as fervently as we pray and love their children just as much as we love our children -- if we considered these things before allowing our leaders to lead us into battle, perhaps we might not go to war in the first place! If that is too large and loving a thought for us to manage in our minds, at least let us consider how, in our common daily relationships, we might live more patiently and constructively with others. Consider what could happen if we were to remember that they, too, have their prayers and that they may be praying for the same things for which we hope and pray.

That person who is being so obnoxious and making life so difficult for us has the same problems and possibilities, the same dreams and fears, the same desires to find love and acceptance as do we. They may be praying, even as we pray, to be their best and do their best and realize their best dreams. How different our lives might be -- and how much better our world might be -- if we were to remember that there are many languages of prayer and that all kinds of people in all kinds of places are constantly praying and laying their hopes and fears and dreams and dreads before God's throne!

One night before our son, Dwight, went back to Saudi Arabia for another year's work, we were over in Detroit for a family gathering. I was at the supermarket buying some groceries for a special supper. It was a cold, crisp, late November evening, and snow was on the way. As I came out of the store, I saw a man and woman shivering near a pay phone, trying to place a call. They were shabby, homeless, street people, lugging all their possessions in large plastic bags. Two men about my age stood nearby, smoking cigarettes, watching them, and making derisive comments about how the world would be better off without such human trash. When I got home, I took out of my notebook of daily contemplative readings a piece about prayer which I have come to cherish. It reads like this:

"There is no one of my brothers ... I can do without ... In the heart of the meanest miser, the most squalid prostitute, the most miserable drunkard, there is an immortal soul with holy aspirations, which deprived of daylight, worships in the night. I hear them speaking when I speak and weeping when I go down on my knees. There is no one of them I can do without ... I need them all in my praise of God. There are many living souls but there is not one of them with whom I am not in communion in the sacred apex where we utter together the Our Father."

There are many languages of prayer, and we are never alone in our prayers. If anything, when we pray we become again part of the great family of God's children -- the family of lost, longing little children whom God sent Jesus to seek and save and bring back home. In the realization that God's great and loving heart hears all of our prayers, let us so pray and let us so live.

🍂

Heaven Can Wait*

January 31, 1993

Scripture Lessons: **Ephesians 2: 1-7; Colossians 3: 1-4; Revelation 21: 1-4.**

Driving home from Michigan during the first week of this month, our car passed a large double tractor trailer. It was not owned by a motor freight company, but by the company that manufactured the product that was being transported. The sides of both trailers were emblazoned with the name and logo of the company. At first, my reaction was that it was rather sobering to be driving 65 miles per hour and passing a truck carrying this particular product. The letters on the trailer read: "Batesville Casket Company." However, whoever designed this advertising had a good sense of humor. The letters on the rear doors of the van read, "Please Drive Carefully -- Heaven Can Wait."

I think there was a movie by that name, and much earlier, back in the 40's, a love song, "Heaven can wait, this is paradise...." Passing over those memories, my sermon-addicted mind quickly called up two statements stored somewhere in the database of my brain. One was a remark of William Wilberforce, the English statesman who was such a vigorous opponent of slavery; the other was a comment about the incarnation of Christ from the writings of G. K. Chesterton. Early the next morning, an outline for this sermon fell quickly into place, and it was constructed around what seems to me to be the odd fact that some of the people who have lived closest to God in this world have, somewhat ironically, been the very people who believed that heaven can wait.

Let's think about two ideas:

THE TRUE SAINTS HAVE BELIEVED THAT HEAVEN CAN WAIT, BECAUSE THEY HAVE BEEN BUSY BUILDING SOME HEAVEN ON EARTH FOR OTHERS.

William Wilberforce, a person of privilege who could easily have spent his life enjoying the perks of his position, chose instead to make his life a battle against the evil of slavery. Through his tireless efforts, slavery was banished from all the territories that were then within the British Empire. He suffered terribly in reaching this goal, but his tribulations were rewarded with success. A pious Christian lady once asked him, "Mr. Wilberforce, is your soul saved?" He answered her, "Madam, I have been so busy trying to save the lives of others that I have forgotten that I had a soul to save."

There is a theological debate represented in this interchange between the pious lady and Wilberforce, and that debate is still going on in the church today. It is the debate over whether the church's business is to save souls or whether the mission of the church should focus upon the saving of the whole person. Am I supposed to save your soul, or is it my ministry and mission to save the whole of your life?

You see, some preachers and their congregations believe that saving souls and sending those souls to an "up there" heaven is the sole business of the church. What they believe is that, at the center of every human life, there is an invisible spiritual core called the soul. Listening to such preachers, you are confronted with the idea that this soul is presently imprisoned within a temporary and imperfect physical body, that the life of the soul within this body is engaged in a contest in which the soul is running an obstacle course that will test and purify it. The body is earthy and subject to carnal sins and appetites; the soul is made for the higher delights. The object is to resist the earthward drag of the body until finally, by the blessing of death, the redeemed soul is released from this bodily prison to float freely heavenward.

Although, as can be shown, this dualism of soul and body is not Biblical, there are all kinds of hymns, prayers, and sermons in which this heretical notion has been fostered. In the saccharin gospel hymn *Sweet Hour Of Prayer* (which, thankfully, was not included in our major Presbyterian hymnals of 1933 and 1990), there was the closing line:

This robe of flesh I'll drop, and rise
To seize the everlasting prize.

That is not a Biblical doctrine; it was a pagan idea, promulgated by Greek philosophers, which made its way into the early church in the form of the Gnostic heresy. Even though this dualism of soul and body was recognized as early as the second century to be heretical, it continues to be fostered today as Christian by those supposedly Biblical Christians who insist that the real business of the church is not that of saving the world, but that of saving souls and thus sending people to heaven. In this faulty conception of faith, heaven can't wait -- everything else can wait! All kinds of ills, evils, and injustices under which people suffer must be ignored lest the church be deterred from the real business of saving souls.

The Bible knows no distinction between your soul and your body. In the Hebrew mind which dominates both Old and New Testament scripture, "soul" indicates the unity of the entire person. Hebrews did not think of themselves as having separate souls and bodies; instead, because God had "breathed the breath of life" into the first person, he became a "living soul," a complete person. The idea of a perishable body that weighs down an immortal soul is simply not Biblical. It is a pagan notion, which invades one of the apocryphal, deuterocanonical books, The Wisdom of Solomon.

This is why, in the Judeo-Christian tradition, obedience to God involves reverence for the welfare of the whole person. This is expressed in the minute detail with which the laws of the Old Testament are concerned with the whole of life: with the physical welfare of all persons, with the rights of the poor, with the concerns of strangers and slaves -- even with the welfare of animals, both domestic and wild animals. The Bible is very physical, earthy, and worldly in its concern. The Old and New Testament scriptures know nothing of a spirituality that is limited to the concerns of a separate and isolated soul.

And this concern for the whole person becomes a special concern of the church in the New Testament. If you question this, you need only consider the scene of the last judgment (Matthew 25) in which the measure of our love for God is judged in terms of our practical care for persons who are poor, hungry, naked, sick, outcast, or in trouble; in today's terms, people on welfare and in jail: the whole person, not just the soul!

How could we possibly think of people as separated entities, as separable body and soul? And how could we ever think that we might justify neglecting the wide range of their human needs -- physical, social, emotional, financial, political -- while concentrating instead upon their souls?

Can you imagine that the people who must live in the hell holes of the earth want us to come and save their souls? And can you believe that somehow we might tell them that their needs can wait for some blessed future day when we will all be reunited in heaven? Can we believe that we ourselves could possibly enjoy being seated side by side forever in heaven with people whose needs we have sought to evade and escape on earth -- many of whom we won't even sit side-by-side with here on earth? That kind of Christianity is a lie! For centuries it allowed people to tolerate the evil of slavery and countless other brutalities and injustices while the church majored instead in the saving of souls.

There is no soul that can be treated separately, as though disconnected from the totality of the entire person. Because of that, the mission of the church must be directed at the entire range of human experience. There is no heaven above that must be allowed to distract us from the hells that exist on earth. And that is why the true saints have believed that heaven can wait, because they have been too busy building some kind of heaven on earth for those for whom life on this earth is a kind of hell. Right on, William Wilberforce, for telling that pious lady "Madam, I have been so busy trying to save the lives of others that I have forgotten that I had a soul to save."

However, there has been an inner and secret source of strength for the life of service that such true saints have carried on in the world.

THE TRUE SAINTS BELIEVE THAT HEAVEN CAN WAIT, BECAUSE
THEY KNOW THAT THEY MUST FIND HEAVEN WITHIN THEMSELVES.

The other statement that came to me when I passed that truck from
Batesville was a comment about the incarnation of Christ from the
writings of G. K. Chesterton. It was something that he had written
about Christ's entrance into the world and of how that story affects
us when its meaning makes its way into our hearts. Because it is a
story about little people and of how the turning point of world history
came without fanfare, and so very quietly, in a small stable in a shabby
corner of the world, Chesterton said this about its inner, personal
meaning:

"It is rather as if a man had found an inner room in the very
heart of his own house, which he had never suspected; and seen a
light from within. It is as if he found something at the back of his
own heart that betrayed him into good."

It's something that I've said before: although some sermons suggest
that Christ is outside of our hearts and lives, trying to gain entrance, it
could just as well be that Christ has been inside our hearts all along,
waiting to be found. If Jesus is, as the Gospel of John indicates (1:9)
"The true light, which enlightens everyone...," then Chesterton
may be on target when he describes the discovery of Christ as the
experience of suddenly coming upon a secret room at the inner core
of one's being. There's a sense in which we all dream of and
desire some quiet sanctuary that is uniquely our own place -- just as
Eliza Doolittle sang, "All I want is a room somewhere...." Perhaps
we all seek for such an inner sanctum, a little heaven within ourselves.

I don't mean a heaven of our own making; I mean the heavenly
center that God has created and placed at the center of every life, a
center that lies undiscovered, where Christ awaits our recognition.
It's like finding that "room somewhere" of which we've always
dreamed, that inner room at the very heart of our own house, which
we had never suspected was already within us.

Those who discover this secret sanctuary, this inner presence of
Christ, live out of it. This is why they can face incredible difficulties
and challenges without becoming strained and tense, and why they

can carry heavy burdens silently and seemingly without effort. This is why their eyes glow with warmth and why their words are friendly and confident. They are not waiting for some future heaven; they have found their heaven, their place, their center of life. And so, they can make life a bit more heavenly for those for whom the world has become a living hell. And they can live through all their own hells with the patience and calmness of those who have found a resting place -- a "room somewhere."

Let me share with you a story from my past. When I was only eight years out of seminary (a callow youth, preaching to fewer than a hundred people a Sunday), there was a prominent preacher who believed in me and gave me a wonderfully encouraging, one-time opportunity. Back in those days -- it was 1961 -- Dr. Theodore Cuyler Speers was chaplain of the Cadet Chapel of the United States Military Academy at West Point. He had had a brilliant ministry at Central Presbyterian Church in Manhattan and had come to the Academy for the final years of his ministry.

And so it came to pass that he heard me speak at a Lenten luncheon for officers' wives that he happened to attend. It also happened that, on a Sunday in January, he was to be away from the Cadet Chapel pulpit, and so he invited me to come to West Point and preach at both morning services. It was a wonderful kindness to a boy preacher, surely the most exciting thing I had ever done in my ministry. I preached to a combined congregation of over 2,000 cadets and officers with General William Westmoreland, then Superintendent of the Academy, sitting in the front pew.

I say it was a wonderful kindness; it renewed my confidence in my preaching ability, and taught me that, if you work hard at sermon preparation, you can preach without fear to any multitude of people. It made me believe in my ability to succeed as a preacher, even though I hadn't. And it also made me promise myself that, as I grew older, I would always try to encourage young preachers and that, when the time came, I would step aside and make way for one of them to stand in my place. Anyway, here is my point. Speers took me into a very small, dark, wood-paneled study off the chancel. What I couldn't figure out was how one got into the sanctuary from this room, which was lined with bookcases. When I asked, he replied, "Ah, that's the trick." With that he touched one of the bookcases in just the right place, and it turned upon some secret hinge and opened onto the magnificence of that huge Gothic sanctuary.

I have come to believe (and it is a belief that changed the whole shape of my ministry) that, inside of every life, there is a secret door, which opens upon much more than just a "room somewhere." It opens upon an enormous sanctuary of inner spiritual splendor. This is not to deny the sinful, fallen condition of human nature, and it is not to say that all people are inherently angelic. Quite the contrary, some people become evil and demonic. But it is to say that, because we are created in the image of God, there is an undiscovered core of imprisoned splendor at the secret center of every life which, by the grace of God, awaits a moment of awakening. For the many people who are seeking their freedom and the fulfillment of their dream outside themselves, I would like to be able to tell them that the way out is always inward, that their beautiful dream is locked inside their own heart.

So, what is the mission of the church? Our mission is to be present to people -- spiritually, practically, politically -- in whatever way they need us. It is to be so fully and lovingly present to people in the name of Jesus that, by the grace of God, they find that secret door, which opens upon the inner grandeur that God has placed at the center of every life.

Believing that changes the whole spirit of our ministry. When I preach to people, I preach to the Christ who is already in their hearts waiting to be recognized. I enter a hospital room realizing that Jesus is already there and that he will remain there after I have left. To people who are deeply troubled, I listen realizing that I don't have the answer, that the true answer is within them waiting to be discovered. To forlorn souls who have lost faith in themselves, I speak to them in the faith that Jesus believes in them, that their confidence and self-esteem is locked within them, awaiting realization in Christ.

And all of this gives me strength in the struggles of my own soul, because it teaches me that nothing -- absolutely nothing -- can happen to me that is bigger than what God has placed within me.

Nothing can happen on the outside of my life -- the loss of my worldly goods, the loss of my job, the loss of my loved ones, the loss of my health and my physical life -- that can take from me the grandeur of that inner sanctuary of splendor where my life is hid with Christ in God.

I cannot open that secret door for you. I can only tell you that it's there, and then pray that God will lead you to its discovery. There is no formula, no technique, nor creed to be believed that I can prescribe as the sure way for finding it. The best thing in life is, finally, a mystery of God's grace, the mystery of your own inner splendor in Christ.

* *This sermon is a revised version of two sermons. Portions of it were contained in a previous sermon preached on September 25, 1988, entitled "The Imprisoned Splendor."*

$\mathcal{A}$ Friend for Every Time and Place

Easter Sunday, April 11, 1993

*Scripture Lesson: **Luke 24 (Selections).***

COMMENTS ON THE LESSON

$\mathcal{A}$lthough we will be reading only one section of Luke's Easter Day narrative, I hope that you will, on your own, take time to read the entire 24th chapter of the Gospel of Luke. If you do that, several distinct features can be observed.

- In Luke's account, all of the appearances of the risen Jesus occur in or near Jerusalem. This is compatible with what we noted last week: Luke's writings have a special affinity for, and interest in, Jerusalem.

- Also to be noted is the fact that, in Luke, all of the appearances of the risen Christ are related as having taken place in one day. This is very different from what Luke will tell us at the beginning of his second volume, the Acts of the Apostles. In that account (Acts 1: 3), a period of forty days elapses between the resurrection and the ascension, and during that interlude, the risen Jesus makes numerous appearances to his disciples. Did Luke change his mind about the facts upon the basis of later, additional information? Or are we to read his account in Acts as an expansion upon the brief, compressed account in his gospel?

- In keeping with his high regard and respect for the faithful women who followed Jesus during his ministry, Luke gives these women a prominent place in his Easter story. When they discover the empty tomb, they are not treated simply as messengers, but as disciples; and their belief in the resurrection certainly shames the disbelief of the eleven apostles who reject the good news of resurrection as an idle tale (24:11).

Our attention is upon the center section of Luke's account (24:13-35) It is a beautifully told story of how the risen Jesus manifested himself to two dejected disciples who were headed home to Emmaus on the evening of the first Easter. Even though they have heard the women's story of the empty tomb and of the angelic confirmation of the resurrection, still they do not believe. Instead, they are going home upon the supposition that the hopes that they had held in Jesus as Messiah had now been dashed to pieces by his execution.

A mystery surrounds their identity. Only one of them is given a name: Cleopas, a name found nowhere else in the New Testament, unless perhaps this is the man with a similar sounding name, Clopas, who is the husband of one of the women who are gathered at the foot of the cross in John's gospel (19: 25). We cannot be sure. We cannot with certainty identify Cleopas. We can only say that he was some disciple within the larger company of Jesus' followers and that his name was, evidently, so familiar to Luke's readers that there was no need to identify him. But who was the other unnamed disciple walking along the road with Cleopas? Not one hint is given, unless we are to assume that it was Cleopas' wife. When they get to their destination, and say to the stranger who is walking with them, "Stay with us . . . ," such words could be read as those of a married couple inviting a stranger to spend the night in their home.

Whoever they were, this stranger who has joined them along the road, and who has explained the death of Christ in light of the prophecies of Hebrew scripture -- this stranger accepts their invitation. As they sit down to dine, he suddenly usurps the role of host, takes bread, blesses and breaks it. Immediately, with eyes of faith, they know that it is the same Jesus who has often broken bread with them. It is Jesus and he is alive.

Perhaps this account has been shaped as a confirmation of the worship of the primitive church. It is set on Sunday, the new day of worship for Christians, and it involves the interpretation of scripture and the observance of a common meal. As such, it carries the promise that the risen Jesus will continue to meet with us in both word and sacrament.

However, its promise is even wider in scope, because this story assures us that the living Jesus is with us on the daily road of our life. Luke loves stories that happen on the road. The pivotal story of the conversion of the Ethiopian eunuch (Acts 8: 26-40) takes place along the road from Jerusalem to Gaza. And, of course, Luke's number one favorite story, the story of Paul's conversion, takes place on the road to Damascus. Luke wants us to know that the living Jesus is with us on every road, opening to us the truth of scripture, and that he is also our host at every common meal, breaking and blessing our daily bread.

SERMON

Let me begin this short sermon for Easter Sunday with some sentences in a letter written by our daughter-in-law from Saudi Arabia. It was written at the beginning of the Moslem season of Ramadan, a season of fasting in which faithful pilgrims from all over the world flock to their holy place, Mecca, which is about 50 miles from their home in Jiddah. It is an interesting sharing of the feelings of a Christian woman who writes from the heartland of Islamic fundamentalism where, imprisoned in the kind of coercion characteristic of all fundamentalisms, everyone must do things their way. Christians cannot engage in public worship. A woman must be properly veiled when outside the American compound and cannot so much as hold her husband's hand in public. This is what Esmina was feeling:

"We're now planning our trip to Spain and Portugal ... I can't wait. I do miss the simple things like holding Dwight's hand in public. Ramadan starts today.... You should see the Africans, Ethiopians and other Muslims that have filled the city for this holiday. Include us in your prayers. It's a weird feeling not being able to give thanks to the Lord Jesus Christ for our blessings in a holy place -- but in my heart, I know God is with us."

Have you ever noticed the interesting fact that Christianity has never become a religion that is big on holy places or holy lands. Although what we call the Holy Land is a sacred piece of earth in Judeo-Christian history, making pilgrimages to that holy place has been a peripheral part of Christian faith and worship. You can be a consummate Christian, completely committed to Christ, mature in knowledge, active in service, radiant in devotion without ever making a pilgrimage to the Holy Land.

A fixation upon the geography of Christianity is more the stuff of the medieval crusades or the promotional preoccupation of preachers who, as a lucrative moonlighting sideline, develop Christian travel and tour agencies. Participation in pilgrimages to Palestine has not been a principal preoccupation of the Church of Jesus Christ.

If anything, Christians have tended to baptize and sanctify all kinds of places all over the world as their holy places. Before going to Jerusalem, Presbyterians, following the trails of Knox and Calvin, might far more likely make their way to Switzerland or Scotland. Depending upon one's theological and denominational heritage, what is the "Holy Land" can be defined differently. Even with this larger number of holy places, robust, healthy Christianity has never depended upon one's ability to get to some place "off there" where it all began "back there." The great moments of faith are not located at some other time or some other place. The resurrection of Jesus Christ has made Christianity a "here and now" faith. The living Lord Jesus Christ is just as much here today as he was there yesterday. That's what we mean when we affirm that Jesus is alive and well. He is not a memory. Jesus is our living Lord and Savior, a friend for every time and place.

Of course, it is always tempting -- even if we're not into the Holy Land thing -- to locate him in some other time and place. It's almost impossible not to do so, especially on a holy day like today. Certainly, at Easter, our minds go back across the years to other churches and other places; to other pastors, other teachers, and other Christian friends. We remember the times when all our loved ones were about us: the days when we got the children ready for church in their Easter outfits, or the times when we were children and sat in the family pew with our parents or grandparents. But now, they're gone. Our children are grown and gone, or our spouse may be gone, and our parents and grandparents may have passed on. It is terribly tempting to think that those were better times, that God was more present back there than here now.

But Easter rescues us from the heresy of such nostalgia, because its message is that Jesus is always here with us in the present day. As in that lovely story of the first Easter evening, Jesus is our traveling companion along every road, even the ones that pass through dark valleys where we must travel alone, bereft of that one special person in all the world whom we loved more dearly than life itself. He still gladly enters any and every humble home when it is toward evening and the day is far spent. He makes himself known to us in the breaking of bread. Whenever we eat, we must always set an extra place for him. And best of all, wherever we may be, he is present in our hearts, setting them aflame with the truth and beauty of his words. He is in our hearts, even when we cannot feel or sense his loving presence -- even when we feel condemned by others or depressed by our downfalls. The living Jesus is with us here and now; he will never leave us or forsake us. That is what Easter is all about.

So, wherever we are and wherever we go in the days and years of all our tomorrows, there will never be a time or place where we cannot hold his hand. Even if we let go, Jesus will never let go of us. The Lord is risen! He is risen indeed! Alleluia!

Which Voice Shall I Follow?

June 20, 1993

*Scripture Lesson: **John 10: 1-18.***

Someone asked me the other day if, in my retirement, preaching would be easier because of having a large barrel of old sermons from which to draw. In answering, I told them something important that I learned about the nature of sermons over 30 years ago.

Back in 1961, I was invited to be part of a small team of preachers who would represent the Synod of New York in a week-long preaching mission to the Presbytery of Puerto Rico, which back in those days was related organizationally to that Synod. We would be assigned to churches in cities and villages around the island. We would preach at least once each day at evening services through translators; however, we were to be prepared to preach on other occasions also. Thus it was that, in our orientation for this mission, we were told to bring along some extra sermons, beyond the basic seven, for what might be expected of us. So, we all set out to locate, somewhere in our sermon barrel, our fourteen best sermons for export to Puerto Rico.

I can still remember the evenings that I spent going through piles of sermon manuscripts from those first eight years of my ministry. It was all I could do to locate even seven that would be suitable for export, and that experiment taught me something about the nature of sermons. It taught me that a good sermon is not just something on paper (although some are no more than just that). Instead, a good sermon is something that happens between a preacher and a congregation. It is a live event in which a preacher communicates where he or she is to a people where they are. And that is why you cannot just take old sermons out of the barrel and preach them over and over again without a substantial amount of revision. A sermon preached at one time and one place to one congregation cannot, without careful and thoughtful revision, be exported to another time and another place. And when the sermon is to be exported to another country and another culture, it becomes all the more difficult to reuse an old sermon.

Answering that question and remembering that experience got me thinking about the subject of exported and imported Christianity. In many nations of the world, Christianity is an imported product. It is something that was exported from other countries and imported into their country.

Are we aware, however, of how confusing it must be to persons from other nations and cultures -- persons who visit America from countries where the Christian faith is still thought of as an export product of the Western world -- to look at the wide and wild variety of export Christianities available in America. If we look at American Christianity with the eyes of people from the so-called non-Christian nations, how confusing the variety must be. It's not the variety of denominations; after all, the mainline ones are relatively friendly to one another. I'm thinking of the diametrically opposite values and viewpoints, which are sold in the name of the same Jesus. A stranger considering the selection of some brand of export Christianity to take home would be confused by the competition between the brands offered.

- As they consider returning to a Third World country that, let us say, is afflicted by poverty, hunger, and massive overpopulation, how does it sound to them to have one preacher telling women that they have no real choice in controlling the number of children they will have, that to exercise certain choices is tantamount to murder, while some other preacher tells them that failure to exercise such responsible choice is to contribute to the starvation of countless children in their overpopulated homeland? And both preachers are speaking in the name of Jesus!

- How does it sound to hear one set of preachers pandering to the very presidents who have condoned the bombing of their homeland and the defoliation of their fields and forests, while other preachers teach that the commandment "Thou shalt not kill" condemns all murder, whether the murder of an individual or the murder of an entire nation?

• What does it say to them to discover that some churches, in the name of Jesus, find polite ways to exclude everyone but those who fit a certain mold and have a certain color skin and keep the recognized rules of respectability, while other churches really proclaim the biblical invitation "whosoever will may come." Isn't it odd that the very churches that most frequently sing the hymn "Just as I am" are the very ones who most frequently exclude certain people who desire only to live their lives "just as they are"?

When you consider the wide and wild variety of ways in which Jesus is represented in American Christianity, wouldn't someone looking in on us from the outside be justified in questioning whether all of these divergent groups are speaking for the same Jesus? Can the same Jesus represent such mutually exclusive values and ideas? When you look at this spectrum of Christian denominations, sects, and cults (all operating in the name of Jesus), which somehow includes everything from the besieged radicalism of David Koresh to the utterly placid, non-controversial comfort of suburban Christianity, something just doesn't make sense. Just because someone opens a Bible and speaks in the name of Jesus cannot mean that he or she speaks for the Jesus of the Bible.

For the next two weeks, we're going to discuss a serious and a sobering question:

Which Jesus do you follow? In today's lesson Jesus says, "I know my own and my own know me ... they do not know the voice of strangers." But how do we know that the voice that we hear and follow is that of the real Jesus? What if we suddenly and finally were to discover that all along we had been following the voice of an impostor and that "our Jesus" wasn't the real Jesus at all? What if, after years of saying that we know him and belong to him, we hear those dreaded words (Matthew 7: 23): "I never knew you." Let's talk today about the inner voices that we hear; next week, about the outer voices.

We are who we are because of the voices that we hear --
voices that tell us who we are.

It doesn't take much training in life to realize that people are who they are because of the inner voices that tell them who they are and how they should operate in life. As you observe the different behaviors of people in a group situation, it becomes clear that people march to the beat of different drummers. Whether it's an office or a club or a church, after we have had time to watch people interacting with one another, we notice that:

- Some people believe that everything that goes wrong is their fault; they can't stop saying "I'm sorry," even when someone else is to blame for the problem in the office. Other people, at the other far end of that spectrum, believe that everything that goes wrong is the fault of others -- everyone else is wrong. They go from job to job, blaming their failure on the betrayal of others or on the "system" or on the world.
- Some people feel a vague sense of guilt even when they can't find anything for which to feel guilty; others are impervious to all feelings of guilt, even when they are very guilty.
- Some people are always suspicious; they suspect that there is always some conspiracy, some catch, some hidden agenda. Other people are too trusting; they have no boundaries and are easily "taken."
- Some people believe that they must never reveal their true feelings; they feel that they must never express their needs or wants or preferences. Others believe that they have a right to wear their changing moods at all times; when they're miserable, the rest of us have to endure their misery with them.

Healthy people are somehow free of these extreme behaviors. They know when to admit honest guilt, but also when the fault is not theirs. They know when to be suspicious of being taken, but also when to be open and trusting. They know when and how to express their feelings, but also when to swallow their grief so as not to be a burden to others. These widely differing behaviors display the fact that we live our lives in obedience to different voices, which speak from down deep within us. I'm not talking about the voices that are heard by deeply disturbed persons. I refer instead to the promptings, urgings, warnings, cursings, or blessings that were implanted within us during our upbringing. The ways in which our parents spoke to us constituted certain signals, and those signals still guide our behavior.

Recently, I was watching and listening to my oldest daughter, Hillie, as she played with her three-year-old son in our backyard. Christopher was collecting sticks from behind the bushes for the purpose of building some kind of hut. As he presented each armful of sticks to his mother for approval, she would say to him, "Oh, Chris, those are really good sticks." When, at last, enough of these good sticks had been gathered, the two of them proceeded to build something like the frame for a flimsy fort, which was then covered by an old sheet. It wasn't much of a fort; it lasted for only an hour before a breeze blew it down. However, something far more important than a fort was being built: by words of praise over something as insignificant as "good sticks," a sense of capability and accomplishment was being nurtured. Christopher was being told that he was capable of doing something right. So, if he believes that he can collect good sticks, then he will gain the confidence to try some larger project, and after that, some still larger project.

As I watched and listened, I remembered from many years ago a young husband sitting across from my desk on a Monday morning, telling me of the gradual breakdown of his marriage. The weekend had been a particularly bad weekend. He had been unable to please his wife and fulfill her demands. After a long recitation of his many failures, he remarked, "You know, you can never do anything right!" Did you hear what he said and didn't say? Why didn't he say, "I can never do anything right?" Because people will often reveal the voices that are prompting them by repeating exactly what was said to them as little children. No one had ever told him what good sticks he was collecting, or what a fine fort he was building. Instead, I could hear someone saying to him, "Why are you wasting your time on that?" And then, as he grew up, some parent correcting him, even while he tried to enjoy a game. "What's the matter with you; you're doing it all wrong; why can't you learn how to throw a ball right?" And then later still, "Here, give it to me; I'll do it; you can never do anything right!" That was exactly what he was taught to believe about his capabilities; and here he was, 40 years later, repeating those exact words to me.

Tell them often enough, and they'll come to believe it.

"You'd better be careful; you could get hurt!"

"Your best is not good enough; I expect perfection!"

"You're disgusting; you ought to be ashamed of yourself for doing something like that!"

"I don't care how you feel; stop crying or I'll give you something really to cry about!"

All of these voices convince us that we are not lovable or capable; that there is something dirty or disgusting about ourselves, our thoughts, or our bodies; that we had better keep our feelings to ourselves; that we must be perfect; or that we are a gigantic mistake in a world that cannot be trusted.

But here's the real problem: It's bad enough coping with all of the negative voices, cursings, and promptings laid on us in our childhood; but how much more complicated does life become when we are encouraged to believe that God is the source of those voices? What an insidious thing it becomes when I am taught that it is Jesus who is speaking to me through all of those unloving and hateful voices.

You see, sometimes the preaching of the gospel (the good news) can actually become the proclamation of bad news. The Bible can be used in such a way as to make Jesus the ultimate source of all the bad voices. If you question this, just consider what is happening when some preacher or evangelist, in the name of Jesus, makes statements like these:

• That it's a bad world, that no one can be trusted, and that we had better live defensively, build high walls, and pack a gun. Isn't it interesting, considering the rash of gun-related killings taking place in public schools, how silent the evangelists are about gun control? Thus, by sowing suspicion and remaining silent, Jesus is made an approving voice for our hysterical fears.

• That we ought to be ashamed of our bodies and of our sexuality. By their obsession with sex (as though sexual failures are sins of the highest magnitude) and by never preaching about the sins of greed, many preachers actually reverse the emphasis of Jesus, who showed mercy to an adulteress, but issued repeated warnings about the love of money. But, after all, who wants to preach against greed when you depend upon the wealthy to keep your institution funded or your TV program on the air? So, by emphasis or silence, Jesus is made the voice of our sexual shame as well as the approving voice of our greed.

- That God has a special thing about men and wants his church to be led mainly by them, that there is something less than great about being a woman. By teaching that women are still, like Eve, the temptresses who cause all the trouble and that it is their fault when they are raped or harassed -- by such preaching, Jesus is made the voice that still tells women to stay silently in their place.

- That we must be perfect and live by certain narrow, sectarian standards if we would be the children of God. By demanding conformity to their standards as a proof of our faith, they are telling us that we must earn God's love. Jesus is made the voice behind all of those other voices, which have told us that we must earn love.

What is often called a conversion experience is instead a monstrous confusion of Jesus with all of the negative voices that reinforce the toxic shame that the world has laid upon us. By enlisting Jesus into the service of all their unloving, negative agendas, some preachers and evangelists set people on a lifelong pathway of following a voice that is not at all that of the Jesus of the Bible. The voice of Jesus is being equated with all of the bad voices; people are being called to follow a voice that is not that of Jesus.

What would it be like, at some last day, to discover that all along I had not been following Jesus, but had been misled into believing that Jesus was the justification of all my self-hatred, shame, and consequent hatred and distrust of others? Which Jesus are you following? Are you sure that you have not confused the voice of Jesus with all the poisonous, unloving voices that the world has conditioned you to follow?

So, how can I know that the voice I am following is that of the real Jesus?

There is a very primitive answer to that question. It is inherent in the most ancient rite of the church, the sacrament of baptism. *The true voice of Jesus is the one that we can hear whenever we celebrate the sacrament of baptism.* Whenever we celebrate the sacrament of baptism, we are celebrating the fact that God accepted us as his own dear children before we were even conscious of ourselves, let alone conscious of God. God's love engulfed us before we could understand and believe in God, before we could try to please God and earn his love, before we could even try to gain his attention by any act of our own doing. Baptism is doing. Baptism is the mark of the covenant of grace, the assurance that God has loved and accepted us unconditionally, not because of anything that has earned his love, but simply because he has decided to love us and adopt us as his own dear children. It is his decision, not ours. The only decision that we can make is that of joyfully recognizing the love that has been carrying us since our birth.

You see, in the Reformed tradition, we are not waiting for our children to become Christians. We are not waiting for some day when they will fully understand the faith and make an adult decision (after all, who can fully understand the faith?) and thereby be saved. We are not waiting for them to go forward at some revival meeting. In our tradition, our children are already the children of God's grace.

Baptism

This is why some churches locate the baptismal font at the entrance of the church and celebrate the sacrament there in the narthex. It is so placed to remind us that the moment of baptism was our entrance into the faith. We did not walk into the church by ourselves, but were carried into the faith as helpless, unknowing infants, loved and accepted by the grace of God.

Whenever we celebrate baptism, listen to the voice that speaks out of that sacrament. It assures you that, long before the world laid its heavy guilt trip upon you, and long before all the negative voices began telling you that you were a mistake, that you were disgusting or shameful or useless or incapable or unlovable -- long before all of that, God loved you and accepted you just as you are. He still loves you just as you are and wants to liberate you to become all that he created you to be.

And if some dark voice within you is still saying, "Yes, but I'm not that. You don't know how bad I am and how far I have to go before I even begin to look like a child of God," just know that God knows all of that, but still finds you lovable and capable. Long before Jesus' disciples understood him -- understood so poorly and loved him so lamely that they would betray him -- long before that, he still told them that they were the light of the world. And he is saying that same thing to you. He thinks that you're the greatest, that you are capable of collecting the "really good sticks" for the building of his kingdom. His light is not something to be sought outside yourself, not something that you must earn. God's light is already in you. All you need do is let it shine.

To know this -- that apart from all your struggles and efforts to earn love, that you are already loved and filled with God's light -- is to experience a real conversion. It is not the kind of so-called conversion that, in the name of Jesus, intensifies all of your previous guilt and shame, increases the volume of all of the old negative voices, and isolates you from an inclusive relationship with all of God's children. Instead, it is the liberation of knowing that you are loved by God, that you will always be loved by God, and that nothing will ever be able to separate you from his love. To know that is to be freed to follow the loving voice of Jesus, the voice of the true shepherd of the sheep, the voice that will lead you safely home at last.

How Shall I Know Him?

June 27, 1993

*Scripture Lesson: **Matthew 11: 1-24.***

❧

*B*ack somewhere in my first few years in this pulpit, early in one January, I preached a sermon entitled "The Lost Boy." It was about that very interesting episode toward the end of the 2nd chapter of Luke's gospel -- the story of how the boy Jesus somehow got separated from the caravan in which his parents had travelled to Jerusalem, and of how he was lost for three days. It's a story that highlights the humanity of Jesus and his family. It makes the important point that the humanity of Jesus was not a superhumanity, but that what we understand to be his divinity operated within the limitations of our ordinary life. Like the story literally says, Jesus was lost for three days. His childhood was not unlike our own childhood and our own life. He got lost; we get lost. Life was not perfect for him; life is not perfect for us.

A few days later, I received a letter from a lady in the radio audience. It informed me that my sermon was all wrong; that Jesus was never lost and that he really knew where he was and where his parents were during those three days. Having related all this to me, she brought her letter to a stirring conclusion. She wrote, "Jesus was never lost; if anything, you are the lost boy."

I have left out one important part of her letter. In relating to me the fact that she was sure that I was wrong, her reasoning was fascinating. It was so much more interesting than the letters in which people argue on Biblical grounds. Her argument was based on a higher authority than the Bible. She knew that Jesus was never lost, because Jesus told her so. She informed me that she talked with him every day, and he told me I was wrong! So, who was I to speak against God!

How do you know when you're in contact with the real Jesus? How do you know when the voice that you are hearing is his voice? When I ask that question, I hope you realize that I'm not suggesting that we should actually hear voices, whether the voice of God, or of Jesus, or of deceased loved ones, or of anyone else. When you get to the point where you're actually hearing voices, you probably need more help than I can give you.

However, we all do have inner promptings, certain built-in alarm systems, intuitions, proddings of conscience, different drummers. Call them what you will, but in that sense, we all do live our lives in response to certain voices.

And they're not all inner voices. There are other outer voices to which we respond in our search for the right decisions about our lives. We may trust a certain newspaper, a certain news analyst, a certain therapist, a certain author, or a certain teacher. We have come to trust their voice. It is not that we equate their voice with that of God; but if we were to examine all the parts of our guidance system, we would say that their's is one of the voices that has some authority in framing our decisions.

In particular, if we are Christians, there will be some preacher or teacher, some theologian or spiritual guide, some pastoral caregiver or counselor -- some guru whose teachings, sermons, concepts, or guiding principles have become a voice we have learned to trust. Although we wouldn't go so far as the woman who wrote me the letter -- we wouldn't say that we actually talk with Jesus -- we would say that, in the voice of this mentor of our choice, we think we perceive the mind and voice and heart of Christ. After we have talked with them, or have heard them talk, or have read what they have written, we feel closer to God, more in touch with ourselves.

However, how do you know when your selection of a guiding voice is correct? We began talking about this last week. How do you know when to trust your inner voices? So many of them are dark, negative promptings implanted by our experience in a dysfunctional family (and many so-called Christian families turn out to be very dysfunctional). So many of our guilty, shame-based, suspicious, depressive feelings are the result of a toxic family environment.

This inner confusion can fuel our poor judgment in knowing and selecting the voices outside ourselves to which we will be attentive. And when you have so many preachers, teachers, and evangelists making radically conflicting claims, espousing diametrically opposite values and viewpoints, how can you know who speaks for Jesus?

And so, in these two sermons, we are asking the questions "Which voice shall I follow?" and "How shall I know him?" Scary questions -- but questions worth asking. After all, what would it be like to come to the end of my life and discover that all along I had been following someone other than the real Jesus? What if the lady who wrote to me discovers that it is some other voice to which she has been listening in her little daily talks with Jesus? Or what if I discover, after years of preaching, that I am indeed "the lost boy"?

Well, that was the question John the Baptist was asking when he was alone in prison. When some circumstance imprisons us, cuts us off from our ordinary activity, isolates us from the usual circle of friends and round of life, the doubts that we have kept down deep within us begin to make their way to the surface. And so John asked, "Are you the one who is to come, or are we to wait for another?"

It is interesting that Jesus did not give a theological answer -- well, not in the sense in which so many of us judge whether someone is or is not a real Christian by evaluating the biblical or theological correctness of their beliefs.

Many of us listen for certain buzz words, which tell us whether or not the person under scrutiny believes the correct things. During my years in fundamentalism, we were taught that we could tell who really knew the Lord by the way in which they talked about their faith. True believers would speak of how they "came to know the Lord," and really true ones knew the exact day upon which "Jesus came into their heart." Such language was a certain clue that, if you were to examine them in greater detail, you would find that they believed in the essential doctrines of the faith: the plenary verbal inspiration and inerrancy of the Bible, salvation by faith in the saving efficacy of the blood of Christ, the premillenial second coming of Christ, and the eternal damnation of all who did not believe in those and other essential doctrines -- even if they were the "heathen" in some foreign land who had never heard about them or had the chance to believe in them.

However, we were not coldly doctrinaire in our standards. It wasn't just what you believed; it also mattered how you lived. True believers would not smoke, drink, dance, attend movies, or wear lipstick.

Lest I seem to be one-sided or sarcastic in my analysis, let's notice that even sophisticated Presbyterians to a certain extent have definitions of what is proper belief and lifestyle. We ought not to feel all that superior to the fundamentalists solely on the basis that our various confessions are theologically, biblically, and historically more correct or that our definitions of lifestyle are seemingly less judgmental.

Though it is true that we do not require a theological statement of the rank-and-file church member, we do require more of ordained officers. They have to affirm their general acceptance of the confessions of our church. So, while the content is different, it's the same idea: really true believers accept and affirm certain doctrines.

And though our standards for a Christian lifestyle differ with those of the fundamentalists in not focusing upon or judging certain worldly pleasures or entertainments, still we have some interesting specifics. In our current state of theological-moral gridlock, sexual orientation has become the sine qua non of ordination requirements. Self-affirming, unrepentant, practicing homosexual persons may not be ordained. As in the military services, if you just don't tell the truth about yourself -- if you'll just lie about who you are, you can serve in Jesus' army. All other unrepentant sinners are somehow overlooked.

And, of course, there are all kinds of other doctrinaire approaches for finding out who God's good guys really are. Many arch liberals are really fundamentalists in their demand that their inclusive catchwords be used or that their pet programs for saving the world be affirmed unquestioningly as proofs for demonstrating that one is a true believer. It is very difficult for all of us to disassociate the definition of a true Christian from some defined system of belief or approved form of behavior. How shall I know him?

Jesus gave an interesting answer to the messengers of John the Baptist. It was a Biblical response; it was an intertwining of verses from the Book of the Prophet Isaiah (specifically from 29: 18-19; 35: 5-6; and 61: 1). However, Jesus rearranged them in a particular order of his own choosing. Notice what he did. He said, "Go and tell John what you hear and see: the blind receive their sight, the lame walk, the lepers are cleansed, the deaf hear, the dead are raised. . ." What more was there to say? What more could you want for proof than that the dead are raised?

But Jesus didn't stop at that point in his answer. There was something more convincing than all the healing miracles he had performed; there was something even more impressive than the raising of the dead. What was it? Read the verse again, and notice the progression: the blind, the lame, the lepers, the deaf -- all healed, then the dead are raised. And finally, the greatest of all miracles -- "the poor have good news brought to them." Finally, someone has time for poor people! The sure mark of the Messiah and of those who speak in his name is that whatever they say or do will, in some way, be good news for all the poor, little, forgotten, shoved-aside people of the world. When a preacher values the esteem of the poor more than the favor of the rich, you can be sure that that preacher's voice echoes the voice of Jesus.

And Jesus' answer to John is perfectly consistent with what he says toward the end of Matthew's gospel when he talks about the day of judgment and the basis upon which we will be judged. There is no mention of correct theology or proper lifestyle. Instead, Jesus deals with the gut issues of life: what we have done for the hungry and thirsty, how we have welcomed the strangers and weirdos, how we have clothed the naked, cared for the sick, and visited the prisoners. So, if you want to hear his voice and find his presence in the world, seek out all of those poor souls and love them in the name of Jesus. Look for the people who are neglected, oppressed, or kept in some kind of confining definition. Attend to the people who are shoved aside and not allowed in the mainstream. Seek out the second-class citizens who are denied the rights and privileges granted to the normal people. Look for the people who are pushed off the main road onto the side roads; those are the poor for whom the true ministry of Jesus is good news.

What a hideous heresy it is when some preacher or evangelist boasts that they have decided to "stick to the gospel" and avoid the side issues. There is no gospel that is good news unless it deals with the people on the side roads! Those are the roads that Jesus travelled. When it says that Jesus was a friend of tax collectors and sinners, it means that he made friends with the wrong people, travelled with the wrong crowd, refused to eat at the right clubs with the right people, failed to know where his bread was buttered, and would have been an absolute failure as pastor of a Presbyterian Church or as president of a Presbyterian Seminary. The kind of craven behavior that somehow communicates to the power and wealth of the world that you can be bought and that you know where your bread is buttered -- such a pattern of pandering prophecy was unknown to Jesus. By the world's standards of prudent preaching, he had his priorities all backwards. If Jesus had a theology, it was a theology of always seeking some way of making himself good news for the poor, the side-tracked, the oppressed, the strangers, the prisoners. And that's where the theological tests of orthodoxy fall apart. The choice to align yourself with the poor seems to have little to do with correct belief. I have known people who believe all the wrong things and fail all the tests of proper personal behavior, but who somehow live their lives where Jesus lived his. And I have also known people who believe all the right things and use all the proper buzz words and behave in a balanced manner, but who always find some sophisticated way to evade the sticky issues and wrong people. It just happens that they are always so busy doing the right things that they can never find time to identify themselves with the wrong people.

A dear old fundamentalist friend of mine died recently. He believed all the wrong things about the Bible and about Christian doctrine, and on that level probably prayed for me as an apostate preacher who had gone astray. But he lived a life of deep personal poverty. For years he tried to live on 10% of his income and to give 90% of it away. He was audited frequently by the Internal Revenue Service without ever being found wanting; they simply could not believe that anyone could live so sacrificially.

I have also known of a man who had little or no theology of that kind. He was just a faithful attendant at his Presbyterian church. But he too lived a life of voluntary poverty, confining himself to a tiny cabin in which he slept on a wooden bench. When he died, he left tens of thousands of dollars to the work of Christ.

These two saintly men never met. Theologically, they were worlds apart; but spiritually, they were brothers in their inner freedom and wealth. No one is ever free if they live without concern for those who are oppressed. No one can ever enjoy wealth that they do not share sacrificially with the poor.

If you want to know when you're hearing the voice of the real Jesus in the cacophony of shrill voices that claim to be speaking for him, listen to the quiet lives and simple ways of men and women who make their lives good news for the poor. Forget about correct belief and proper behavior. If the little, poor people of the world love them, and if the big people can't stand them, that will be the sign you're seeking. Such lowly souls are the servants of Jesus. Listen to them.

I heard something beautiful the other night at a service I attended. It was a men's chorus. Some of my favorite music is what is sung by large, Welsh male choruses; it's a frequent community institution in Wales. However, this was not a Welsh male chorus. It was a large, well-trained chorus of gay men. Maybe you don't like even the mention of such a group, but they made beautiful music and in one of their songs, spoke the truth of Jesus. It was a folk-type number, which ended with this thought:

You can be anybody you want to be . . .
But the only measure of your words and your deeds
Will be the love you leave behind when you're done.

In Jesus' definition, true love is the love for which we can expect no return. There are all kinds of people in the world who can reward you substantially for your kindness. But the poor can give back nothing but the love of their hearts. Seek their love, because in their words you will hear the voice of Jesus, and in their love you will experience his love.

❦

The Perfect Teenager

November 14, 1993

Scripture Lesson: **Genesis 2: 4-9, 15-17; 3: 1-9.**

❦

COMMENTS ON THE LESSON

*I*t is not necessary to be a Hebrew scholar to recognize that there are two separate creation narratives in the Book of Genesis. A careful reading of any English language version of the Bible reveals two quite different accounts.

In the first account (1: 1 - 2: 4a), the opening scene has the appearance of a hostile, chaotic, storm-tossed sea. As we view it, we remember that the Hebrews were not lovers of the ocean. In the Hebrew eye, the winds and the waves of an angry sea were not objects of beauty. As creation begins, God restores order to the primeval disorder. Thus, the God of the first creation account is a God of order. Everything about this first account is orderly. With language that is measured and repetitive, God's work is described as a deliberate process in which the world is carefully assembled, piece by piece, and made ready for humanity.

The creation of humanity on the sixth day differs from the previous days, because it necessitates something like a committee meeting, an assembly of the heavenly court. Notice the language (1: 26): "Let us make humankind in our image. . . ." Also notice that male and female are created at the same time and that they are given the task of exercising dominion over the world that God has made (vv. 26 and 28).

In this account everything is orderly and everything is good. At each stage of the process, God seems to compliment himself on what a great job he has done. God's creation ends upon that note, with God viewing all that he has done (v. 31) as "indeed, . . . very good." With such a sense of satisfaction, God takes the next day off (2: 2). As this account ends, there are no problems in God's new world; everything is orderly and in place.

In the passage that we will now read from the second creation account, we are given an entirely different picture of God and his world. For the first time in the Bible, we hear the most personal name for God: Yahweh, rendered in English as Lord God. In marked contrast to the first account, instead of an opening scene of watery chaos, we see what appears as a waterless, lifeless desert (2: 5). From a stream which arises, this barren earth is watered and prepared for planting. With the earth thus prepared, this Lord God, who is more human in appearance than the God of the first account, acts as both a sculptor and gardener. Making clay from the dust of the ground, he forms the first human, breathing into him the breath of life (2: 7), and then plants a garden (2: 8, 9) into which he places this first man. This first man is more lively and human than the orderly obedient creatures in the first account. He is capable of participating with the Lord God in the care of the earth. Instead of exercising dominion over the earth, man's role is to care for ("to till it and keep it," 2: 15) and enjoy God's creation ("pleasant to the sight and good for food," 2: 9).

This new human is someone with whom we can identify. He is capable of obedience, and therefore also of disobedience. That he is given a commandment (v. 7) testifies to the fact that he is a creature of choice. He is also subject to loneliness (2: 18). He is capable of social and sexual intimacy, and for both purposes, God creates a partner for him. Finally, as we learn in the events that follow, God has taken a risk in the creation of such a lively, self-willed creature. Both the man and the woman have been created with the option that they could disobey God. It becomes a fatal option that they proceed to choose (3: 1-7).

SERMON

I think that it is pretty clear to anyone who spends any time thinking about it that we have come to the point where, given some advance planning, parents no longer have to put up with the frustrations of living through the teen years with their children. Now if you already have teenagers, we can't help you; once you've started a family in the traditional manner, it's too late. However, if you plan ahead and build your family with the tools of modern science and technology, you can have perfect teenagers and peace of mind through those years when your neighbors -- those who are raising traditional teenagers -- are going absolutely bonkers.

It is quite obvious from what is happening in various high-tech industries that we can now build a perfect teenager. With the great advances that have been made in the science of robotics, the day has arrived when we can, given a considerable investment, construct a worry-free teenager. Granted, the price right now is quite high. However, when the idea catches on, as is always the case with new technology, prices will be coming down, and the product will be even more refined. Nonetheless, even at today's high price, when you consider what you will be getting for your money, you should think carefully about getting in on the ground floor before the idea takes off.

What we can build for you right now is a teenager programmed to perfection. In fact, you can pick and choose from a wide variety of options. Don't get the idea that all of the robotic teenagers will be the same. Though all of them will be worry-free, with guaranteed relief for you from the usual hassles, in other ways they will be exactly what you have always wanted in a teenage daughter or son.

All of them come with the standard hassle-free software package at no extra charge. Included in this package are such features as:
- They never talk back or argue. The only questions that they ask are those which clarify a command that their system cannot process.
- They always do their homework without being asked, and it is done to perfection. Thus, your perfect robotic teenager will always be at the top of his or her class in middle or high school and consequently will gain immediate acceptance into the college of your choice -- get that, your choice. No more arguments about not going to Dad's or Mom's old Alma Mater.
- More importantly, however, there will be no more waiting to get in the bathroom, no more arguments over keeping their room picked up, no more dented fenders or parking tickets (they are the best drivers on the road), no more negotiating the time which they

must be home from the dance, no more pleading with them to mow the lawn, no more demands for a higher allowance, no more screaming scenes over the questionable characters they choose to call their friends. From now on, it will be all quiet on the teenage front!

And if that sounds like heaven on earth, consider the additional pleasure of having them programmed with the vocational and talent aptitudes of your choice.

- Do you want a musical teenager? Just tell us, and we can program one who won't even need to practice. No more listening to those torturous finger exercises; just ask them, and they can play Chopin all through your cocktail hour.

- Do you want a business-management orientation? Just tell us, and we'll build you one who will have the sense to go into the family business, just like you and your father did. The sensible chain of the generations will not be broken by a son who, instead of knowing a good thing, wants to earn a Ph.D. in medieval poetry and live in poverty!

- Do you want a scientific genius, one who can make it big in computers? We can build those too, with the additional guarantee that they won't be able to deprogram themselves. No more changing their minds and setting off in harebrained directions!

When you think about all of this, and the centuries it has taken to arrive at this point in the development of technology, and especially about the generations of parents who have suffered through the teen years with their children, what comes to mind is a theological question. It goes like this: If God, who knows everything, and has known since the beginning of time that his human creatures would someday figure out how to build computers and robots (because, you see, God built into our minds the very aptitudes by which we were able to develop artificial intelligence systems) -- if God knew all of this from the beginning, why didn't he do a better job in building people? Why did God create teenagers? Why did he construct a human animal that passes through such an impossible stage on the way to its mature shape and form? After all, if God has given us the brains to build computers, why didn't he build a human being who is born little and cuddly, but grows and matures in a hassle-free process of development?

When I asked this question, it opened up a whole new view of the creation stories in the Book of Genesis. Granted now, these are mythical, theological stories, which are not told to tell us how the world and its creatures came into being, but to make a statement about why we are here. Granted that, I saw something new in my imaging of the story.

I had always pictured the first man and woman in a state of mature physical development. When I tried to make a movie in mind of that fabulous sixth day of creation, I had always pictured the man and the woman as in their late 20's or early 30's, looking like the kind of couple who eat a low-fat diet -- rich in beta-carotene, never drink anything stronger than Perrier™ water, and use their NordicTrack twenty minutes every day. My vision of our original parents is one of utter physical beauty and vitality. And my guess is that you also picture Eden in that same manner. These are not older folks who are beginning to look dumpy; neither are they innocent children on the eve of their first day at middle school.

If you read the story carefully, however, they behave like teenagers. It reads as though God started the human drama by placing two teenagers in a garden. Their behavior is that of the quintessential, classic teenager. Just look. They are old enough to be left alone without a baby-sitter. They are at that point, as we say, where we ought to be able to trust them to be responsible -- or so we thought. They are given a garden of good stuff to enjoy. Just look at all we have given you! All we are asking is that you not -- repeat not -- eat of the tree in the midst of the garden, the tree of the knowledge of good and evil. That is the one simple rule for the day: don't even touch it, don't even think about eating of that tree. Got it? Right? Wrong! We're hardly out of the house before they get talked into trying the one thing we've told them not to try. Why do they listen to other people and their "smart" friends? Why do they try thinking for themselves? Why listen to that serpent?

And, of course, God doesn't come off all that well in the story. Having created a human animal with such teenage propensities, he acts like the quintessential and indecisive parent of such teenagers. He doesn't carry through on his threats. God is not consistent in the enforcement of his rules. He tells them that, on the day they eat of that forbidden fruit, they will surely die. But they don't. Something dies in their relationship with God, but there is at least a partial truth in what the serpent tells them: they do not surely die.

Instead, God, like a parent who persists in loving impossible teenagers, goes looking for them. If God had had some parent assertiveness training in good tough love, he would have left them lost and wandering out there in the woods. Instead, like a victim of his own overindulgent parental soft love, he goes looking for them.

Why not give up on them? Why not start out all over again and make some real people who have some mature common sense and who act like grownups? Instead, it takes the rest of the Bible to tell of the age-long search for God's lost lambs. The Bible reads like the story of the typical household in which the parents are not in control of their teenage children. God keeps warning them, and they keep on disobeying. God keeps on forgiving them, and they keep on abusing God's forgiveness. God is a prisoner of his own forgiving love. God has programmed them for failure, and with certain notable exceptions, they fail. But God keeps on forgiving them and hoping that they will grow up some day.

What is clear is that God created teenagers -- a whole world of teenagers. And through all the years of our lives, we go on acting like teenagers. Even when we grow up to be parents, we go on (we won't admit it) acting just like our teenagers, making the same mistakes over and over again until our dying day.

However, let's thank God for the way the story has gone, because that story of our failure and God's forgiveness is good news. What do I mean? Think about two things:

WITHOUT THE GIFT OF FREEDOM, WE COULD NEVER ENJOY A LOVING RELATIONSHIP WITH GOD

Freedom of choice was written into our story from the beginning. From the first day of our creation, we were creatures who had the capacity for making decisions. When God told those first two teenagers that they were not to eat of the forbidden fruit, it was obvious that they were creatures who must make the decision to obey. They must choose to be in a relationship of loving obedience with God. They possessed the freedom to choose, and the freedom to choose is, by definition, the freedom to make the wrong choice. God built this freedom to fail into the very nature of the human animal. And isn't it grand!

Think about it. Suppose God from the beginning had done it right; that is, in terms of modern technology. What if God had built the perfect robotic teenager -- one that was programmed with all the good options that I described at the beginning of this sermon? There is one thing that such a perfect teenager could never give you. You can program perfect performance and unwavering obedience to programmed instructions, but you can never program love. You cannot enjoy a loving relationship with a machine. Love can exist only between two unpredictable persons who, in utter freedom, have chosen to love one another. But of course the freedom to choose to love is, by definition, the freedom to choose not to love. Because we are what we are, creatures of choice, we can love one another with hearts that pulsate with love and passion; however, with that same freedom, we can hurt and reject one another and break the heart of the one whose love we spurn. Our freedom to choose to love makes life a risky business. We can control a machine, but we can never experience love without the terrifying risk of being heartbroken.

But God took that risk. Instead of devising perfectly automated bipeds who would behave in a predictable manner, God took the risk of creating perennially teenage humans. God took the risk because he wanted children who could love him for no other reason than that they chose to love him.

You cannot command love, and you cannot control love. You can only receive love as a gift, which another human being chooses to give you. The perfectly programmed world would lack the one quality that makes the world go 'round. It would be devoid of the greatest ability that God has built into the heart of our being: the freedom that makes loving relationships possible.

Some people choose not to have children. Some choose not to

have even a dog or cat. Though more controllable, not even dogs or cats are perfectly controllable. If you want perfect control, don't let any living creature into your life. Avoid as much as possible any and all contact with living creatures. Your heart will never be broken; but neither will you ever know the greatest gift of all, the gift of love.

So give thanks for all the impossible hassles of life: the hassles with children, with spouses, with parents, with friends and enemies, with neighbors near and far, with people at work or at play, and with dogs and cats. To live in a world in which love is possible, we must accept the possibility of people who are impossible. However, even those people can change.

So give thanks for a second gift: that, in addition to freedom, God has also built the possibility of forgiveness into our world. Without the freedom to fail, we could never become the children of God. We must also add that:

WITHOUT THE GIFT OF FORGIVENESS, WE COULD NEVER ENJOY A GROWING RELATIONSHIP WITH GOD

Just as the possibility of failure was written into our nature from the moment of creation, so, too, was the possibility of forgiveness. And, as we have already noted, the story of the Bible is the story of how God has been the prisoner of his love for his children and of how he cannot stop forgiving them, granting them endless chances, and hoping for their growth and improvement. What a marvelous commentary this is upon our human nature.

It is one thing that God has given us the freedom to choose. That freedom gives us the choice to live in love. But it is just as grand to know that God grants us endless forgiveness. That tells us that we are capable of repair and restoration. Think of what that says about every person walking the face of the earth, regardless of how hopeless and unpromising they may seem, or of how evil they may seem to have been. Everyone you will ever meet has possibilities for growth. Everyone you will ever know can be changed and made new. We can always be "fixed" and renewed. At any point in our life, we can start all over again. And how wonderfully true that is of our own young people.

They may not be perfect, but how they can grow, and how they can change! On one day, you wonder if they'll ever grow up; then, all of a sudden, there they are, far beyond where you ever thought they'd be. On another day, you're about to despair over the mess they've made of things. Then again, all of a sudden, they've made a U-turn and by some power of grace abounding, they are changed persons.

As I wrote this sermon, my mind went back to the years when our twin sons were in high school in Michigan. Late one afternoon, we had a call from the police telling us to come right away. Our Dwight had had an accident driving home from school. There were lots of dirt roads in the suburb of Bloomfield Hills, where we lived, and on one of them, Dwight, had gone into a bad skid, spun off the road, and hit a tree. We sped to the scene of the crash, which was only a short distance from our home.

What we saw would almost paralyze a parent with terror. There were police cars and fire trucks. The family station wagon was a mangled mess. The left rear end, right where the gas tank was located, had slammed into the tree and had been crushed. Somehow, miraculously, the spurting gasoline had not ignited; and there, in the midst of all this wreckage, stood Dwight and his passenger friend, alive and unscathed.

After signing some papers and answering some questions, we walked back to our other car to head home. The station wagon was not a new car, and I was pretty sure that because of its depreciated value the insurance coverage would not be large enough to allow the purchase of a new wagon. This was going to cost us some money. I held my tongue and waited awhile before asking how this accident had happened. It seems that my gentle, nature-loving son had made a quick decision to hit the brakes and swerve to avoid hitting a rabbit. I still held my silence. I was trying to picture this $2,500 rabbit hopping happily through the woods and meadows of Bloomfield Hills. Before I could say a word more, Dwight said, "I'm really sorry,

Dad. Maybe we could sell my new skis to help pay for this."

What strange decisions they make as they grow up! But then, too, with what wonderful surprises they bring you to tears of joy!

So, thank God for these young people of our church family. Be thankful that they have their moments of failure. How else will they ever learn and grow? And when they do fail, give them endless forgiveness. How else will they ever experience the grace to change? Just make sure that you have forgiven yourself for your own past failures. Make sure that you're not taking out on them your frustrations over your own past. Be sure that you're not passing on to them your inability to forgive yourself. Give thanks to God, who gives us freedom to fail so that we can grow, and who also allows us to fall so that, by his grace, we can be lifted up to newness of life in Christ Jesus.

Drawn to the Light

....
January 2, 1994
*Scripture Lesson: **Matthew 2: 1-12.***

There is an honest, up-front question that we should ask before we attempt to say anything about the story of the wise men: we need to ask whether we believe that such a thing really happened. Some of us would not raise that question. This is a story that is so much a part of our faith tradition that we have never thought about questioning its factual basis. For that matter, the visit of the Magi is so much a part of our manger scenery that it seems irreverent, even on strictly literal Biblical grounds, to remove them from our nativity scenes. We don't want to tamper with tradition, even when the tradition denies the New Testament. When I point out that in Matthew's account there is no visit to a manger, our reaction may be: "Please, don't spoil the story for me, even on biblical grounds!" So, we just believe in the story of the wise men. It's a story that has always been there for us.

For others, it's not that easy. If we were not brought up with this tradition, and if our minds have been formed or informed by different disciplines of thought, we may react by pointing out that it is rather difficult for a scientifically literate adult of our day to make any sense of a story in which a wandering star guides oriental astrologers to the birthplace of a child-king. It does read like the stuff of fairy tales. Such a reaction does not mean that we are of little faith and that we might as well give up on ever being a Biblical Christian. It may indicate nothing more than that we are taking this story seriously and thoughtfully. To have no problems with such a story may be a sure sign that we are not reading the Bible carefully. Faithful, Biblical Christians should find this story difficult.

I say that because we cannot read it as it was read by the audience to which the writer of Matthew's gospel addressed it. It is impossible for us to do so, because too much has happened between that day and ours. The Bible was written in a day when the solar system was unknown as it is now understood by modern astronomy. No one knew that many of the stars that we see at night were gigantic suns in comparison with which our sun looks like a tiny speck of a star. The planets had not been viewed with the dramatic closeness with which we have seen them through the lens of advanced telescopic photography. We simply cannot recapture the sense of superstition, mystery, and wonder with which ancient people viewed the heavens. However, we can read their stories sensibly and translate their meaning for our lives.

What we do know is that there was conjunction of the planets Jupiter and Saturn in the constellation Pisces in 7 B.C. Although that is several years before the birth of Jesus, when you consider the common widespread memory of such a happening and combine it with a blending of astrological traditions and a midrashic interpretation of Old Testament texts, you have the makings of what is called a haggadah: a story made up from Biblical materials to make a theological point. Biblical materials for such a weaving would have been supplied by such texts as Numbers 24: 17 -- "a star shall come forth out of Jacob . . ." and Isaiah 60: 3 -- "nations shall come to your light and kings to the brightness of your rising. . ." It is clear that the author of Matthew needed such a story for his congregation. His is a very Jewish congregation, and this is a story that validates the sharing of the gospel with the Gentiles. He needs to reassure the strictest Jewish Christians of his congregation that a mission to proclaim the gospel to the Gentiles was, in fact, foreshadowed in the events that surrounded the birth of the Messiah. From the very beginning, God was seeking the Gentile world, and the Gentiles were seeking Jesus.

What is really interesting, however, is that Matthew dares to tell a story in which astrologers find their way to Jesus. Astrology is not tolerated by Old Testament writers. Though various references "between the lines" make it evident that astrology and other forms of magic and divination held a certain popularity with the common people, it is also clear that the Law and the Prophets (Isa. 8: 19; 44: 25; 47: 13, 14; and Dt. 18: 10-12) condemn all such divination. So the author of Matthew's gospel was telling his congregation something that they really did not want to hear. What was it?

GOD IS NOT A PRISONER OF THE CHURCH

What this story is saying is that God's reach into the world extends far beyond the reach of the church. The arms of God are longer than the arms of the church. God is always reaching out into the world, far beyond the outreach of the church. Indeed, God is always out there in the world ahead of the church. God is there long before the church ever gets there.

When you begin to understand what this story is saying, something interesting emerges. Though we think of this as a beloved part of our Christmas tradition, it may not at all have been a beloved story in the church to which Matthew was writing. Indeed, if they had had their way, they might have wanted to remove it as theologically X-rated material, because it teaches something that orthodox souls never want to hear. It teaches that God has all kinds of ways of drawing people into his presence -- all kinds of ways of leading people to his light, and many of those ways are highly unorthodox.

After all, this is a story about pagan people who found their way to God on what was the wrong road. In this story, God rewards pagan inquisitiveness by using astrological curiosity (an Old Testament "no-no") as a means of leading people to the Christ. It's not supposed to work that way. If we follow the traditional pathways by which people are supposed to find God, then the proper order is that the church is supposed to carry the message to them. After that, if they respond, the church opens the gates to them and receives them into the fold.

It must have been maddening to Matthew's congregation to learn that God can draw people to himself without the help of the church. We need to remember that this was a very Jewish congregation. Christianity was still, for the most part, a sect of Judaism. Thus, it was bad enough that they were being told that they must open up the doors of their church to those Gentiles who wanted to embrace the Christian faith. What this story was saying was that, even if they didn't, God would find his own way to find those who were seeking him. Indeed, this was a story saying that God can find us on any road. It would not be surprising to find a story like this in the Gospel of Luke with that gospel's strong emphasis upon Gentile Christianity. But to find it in the Gospel of Matthew is extraordinary, because Matthew is trying so very hard to establish the fact that the Christian faith was all along anticipated by the Old Testament. In this story, the strict guidelines of the Old Testament regarding astrology are ignored. God is not confined by his own guidelines. God goes beyond the limits of his own established church to seek and find those whom the church is not seeking. And that is, indeed, rather maddening, even for us.

There is, after all, a certain satisfaction in feeling that we are the keepers of the light, that the dark and sinful world outside of the church is dependent upon us for hearing the message, seeing the light, and being allowed to enter the gates of the church. Indeed, many appeals to missionary outreach are made upon the basis of that flattering notion.

We are urged to carry Christ to those in heathen darkness (at home or abroad) upon the supposition that, unless we go, they cannot be rescued from their lost estate. So, if this scenario is played out, on the dreadful day of judgment, those who have not been the recipients of our missionary outreach will be turned away. They will be told that, although their situation is eternally unfortunate, they cannot be saved because the people of Shadyside Church did not carry the gospel message to them. It is a high degree of spiritual flattery to think that we could ever possess such power over the eternal welfare of others. And it is also an extraordinary distortion of God's just nature to imagine that any soul would be lost eternally because of the neglect of some other soul!

Thank God for this story. It reminds us that God is already out in the world seeking his own and that, whether or not we carry the light into the darkness, God's light is already shining in the darkness, drawing those who seek him to themselves. And such an understanding of God corrects our understanding of the outreach in which we engage in the world:

- It means that we go into the world because God is already out there.
- It means that we do not carry Christ into the world; he has gone there ahead of us.
- It means that we speak to the world because God has already spoken.

However, beyond correcting and enlarging our understanding of the church's mission, this story gives us a wonderfully enlarged vision of God's outreaching love to all souls. What do I mean? I mean that, whether we know it or not, God is always reaching out and drawing us to himself. We are not what we are because of our own search for God: we are what we are because God has drawn us to himself. We may think that we have arrived at an understanding of God as a result of our search for him. The real truth, however, is that God has inspired and made possible our journey into his presence. And God is reaching out to and searching for every human life.

After all, can't you remember times when, although you weren't seeking God -- maybe even running away from him, trying to forget him -- when, nonetheless, something was holding on to you, pulling at you, drawing you in another God-ward direction?

Is it like a thin thread, a fragile web, with which God holds on to us, a thread ever so fine that cannot be broken? Is it a voice, silent like a whisper, that cannot be drowned out by all the world's senseless noise? Or do we need some other metaphor? Could it be a force, deep and powerful beyond all reckoning, that we cannot resist forever -- a force that will be drawing us to itself through all eternity.

One of the easiest stars to find in the winter sky is Betelgeuse in the constellation Orion. When you locate it in the left shoulder of Orion the Hunter, it appears as no more than a bright red speck of light when compared to the brightness of our Sun. Actually, it is an enormous red supergiant star, 400-million miles in diameter. If our Sun were as far away as that huge red star -- 500 light years -- our Sun is so small in comparison that it would be invisible to the naked eye at that distance! The stars are good at hiding their true nature, so that what appears as a tiny red point of light is actually a gigantic

Sun, with an awesome gravitational force that consumes the smaller stars that draw near to it.

Is that how we should describe the light and force of God's nature: a heavenly body that appears so very tiny to our worldly eyes, but which, in reality, emits a light beyond our reckoning and a gravitational force that no one can resist forever. Are we actually being drawn to God, however we may resist the tug and pull of spiritual gravity? The light that entered the world at Bethlehem may seem no more than a tiny speck in the limited vision of the modern world, but it is still the light that lightens every life, the mysterious force that tugs and pulls at every heart.

God is seeking us on whatever road we may be traveling, and God can use whatever we may be seeking as a means of drawing us to himself. Just think of the wild, wide variety of stories we could share, if we each told of the strange pathway by which we made our way to the faith: a chance meeting, which changed our whole way of thinking; a book we happened to read, which set our mind off in another direction; some strain of music so beautiful or some sunset so glorious that we had to seek its strange source. God has made himself inescapable. Wherever we turn in the world, there is some hint of his presence, some reminder of his goodness, some echo of his voice, some strain of the music of heaven. God never gives up on us. He follows us down all the pathways that we take, and meets us at every turning.

And if God reaches out with such persistence to draw us to himself, his searching nature tells us what the church should be like in its openness to the world. If the doors of the heavenly city are never shut -- if even in eternity, God continues to await our return -- then the church's doors should never be shut to any seeking soul. Those who are searching for the "something" that they cannot describe should know that the one place in the world where they will always be welcomed is the church. If God's love is endlessly patient in its pursuit of every life, then people should know that the one place where they will never be judged or excluded is the church. Every church should have inscribed over its portals "Whosoever will may come." Sadly, so very many people out in the world have come to realize that the church is, all too often, the one place where they will be judged and where something less than an open door will await them. However, if I have had one controlling objective in my ministry, it is to make the church a clear beacon of the starlight of God's unconditional love.

But if I cannot change the church, I should at least change myself. I can strive to let God's ever-seeking, accepting love and light flow through me. I can try to make myself, like Jesus, a friend of sinners. I can work at becoming the kind of pastor and person of whom those who are seeking the light will be able to say, "I know that Morgan won't ever give up on me; I know that he won't judge me; I know that he'll always find a way to accept me as I am and believe the best about me and hope for the realization of my highest possibilities." We can all strive to be the kind of Christian person who reflects the ever-seeking love of God for every soul on every road. God is not a prisoner of the church. That's what the story of the Magi is about. Instead, God is out in the world, seeking to draw all people to himself. So let's be up and on our camels in all seasons, because God is always calling us to follow his star to the very ends of the earth.

$\mathscr{B}$eginning All Over Again

....

January 16, 1994

Scripture Lesson: ***John 3: 1-16; Ezekiel 36: 24-28; 37: 1-14.***

COMMENTS ON THE LESSONS

$\mathscr{T}$he conversation between Jesus and Nicodemus is often interpreted as the perfect model of "one-on-one" personal evangelism: the kind of conversation in which a zealous Christian witnesses to some unsaved soul about the need to be born again. If we read scripture carefully, it becomes obvious that it is something quite other than that. In the broadest sense, it is evangelistic; it announces the good news. However, it is not a "one-on-one" conversation. When we notice how it is pervaded by plural pronouns, we can see that what was a conversation between Jesus and the old Pharisee, Nicodemus, has been taken onto the stage of a later time. It has been made into a dramatic form of communication by which a congregation of Jewish Christians is speaking to a nearby synagogue congregation of Jews, who are somewhat favorably disposed toward Jesus. Notice how this develops.

Nicodemus begins by saying "Rabbi, we know that you are a teacher who has come from God; for no one can do these signs that you do apart from the presence of God." In these words, Nicodemus is speaking for Jews who, on the basis of Jesus' miracles ("signs"), already believe him to be a prophetic figure. However, that is not enough. The community of Jewish Christian believers for whom Jesus is speaking want their synagogue neighbors to experience that spiritual rebirth "from above" that they have experienced. And let us notice that Jesus is speaking of an experience of rebirth that is "from above." It is Nicodemus who misunderstands what is said and talks of being born "again," as though one might be physically reborn.

Jesus immediately corrects this misunderstanding, making it clear that he speaks of a birth "from above," a spiritual transformation by "water and Spirit." This is an obvious baptismal reference, a clue that this conversation is being staged during the early Christian era when baptism was the sacramental entrance into the church. In other words, this is not a verbatim record of the conversation between Jesus and Nicodemus; instead, it is a later staging of that conversation. A Christian community of faith is inviting a Jewish community of faith to recognize Jesus as Messiah and to receive the gift of the Spirit, which in early Christian expectation accompanied baptism.

This is confirmed by the fact that the language of Jesus employs plural forms. When Jesus says (v. 7) "You must be born from above," he speaks with a plural pronoun, as though he is turning from Nicodemus and speaking to the audience as a group. Having said that, Jesus uses terms that describe the mysterious, unpredictable nature of such a spiritual transformation. Like the wind, which blows where it chooses, this new birth comes to us from outside ourselves and our own effort. We are not the cause of its happening; it comes to us on the winds of the Spirit. As we shall see, this reference has rich associations and meanings for the audience, although Nicodemus is made to seem baffled ("How can these things be?" v. 9).

The staged nature of the conversation between two groups now becomes fully apparent. Beginning with verse 11, it is no longer a conversation between Jesus and Nicodemus. "Verily,...we speak of what we know and testify to what we have seen (the "we" is the Johannine church); yet you ("you" meaning the Jewish synagogue) do not receive our testimony." From here on, the Johannine congregation is making a confessional statement about its essential faith: Jesus is the only one to have descended from heaven (v. 13). Others (Enoch and Elijah) may have ascended to heaven; only Jesus can claim to have descended from above. Next, an unmistakable allusion to the crucifixion is made by reference to the serpent lifted up by Moses in the wilderness (v. 14).

Beyond these very obvious Old Testament references by which

the Johannine church was presenting its gospel to the members of the neighboring synagogue, there is even more powerful Old Testament imagery in Jesus' description of this rebirth from above by water and the winds of the Spirit. The Jewish recipients of this message could hardly have missed such an obvious reference.

Speaking to the exiles who longed for deliverance from their captivity in Babylon, Ezekiel spiritualizes the nature of their captivity and deliverance. By the sprinkling of clean water (Ezek. 36: 25), God will give them a new heart and instill within them his own Spirit, which will make them responsive to his will (vv. 26, 27). Following closely upon this promise, we read Ezekiel's powerful vision of the valley of dry bones and of how the breath (Spirit) of God, coming mysteriously from the four winds (37: 9, 10), brought life to the dry bones ("... they lived, and stood on their feet, a vast multitude"). Those to whom the message of this chapter was being addressed, who were already sympathetic and well disposed toward Jesus as a prophet, would surely have noticed such obvious Old Testament references and images. In Jesus Christ, God's only Son, they were being invited to receive such a mighty rebirth from above -- from death to eternal life (Jn. 3: 16).

SERMON

For the past 35 years, one of my favorite pieces of devotional literature has been a booklet written by the father of world literacy programs, Dr. Frank Laubach. It is a tiny spiritual classic entitled *Letters By A Modern Mystic.* I don't read it every day, but I do keep coming back to it every so often, year after year.

The 47 pages of this booklet are filled with excerpts of letters, which he wrote to his father who lived in central Pennsylvania. Laubach had gone to the uplands of the Island of Mindanao to work with a wild and backward tribe of Islamic people, who looked upon the Christian Filipinos as their traditional enemies. Because of their hostility toward the Christian faith, he did not go there with conversion as his first objective; instead, he went to live among them lovingly and prayerfully, believing that God's Spirit would do its own work in God's own time. With deep respect for their culture, he gave them their tribal life. He taught thousands of them to read, developed industries, fostered health services, and in hundreds of little ways proved himself to be their practical friend. At the heart of this practical work was his own intensely intimate relationship with God. From the moment of his arrival in their midst, his purpose was not to make converts, but in his own life to practice a continual sense of God's presence. Living in the solitude of small quarters, Laubach cultivated a disciplined sense of being fully present with God in every moment -- the sense of living in George MacDonald's "holy carelessness of the eternal now." Believing that any hour of any day could be as full of God as we desire, he practiced filling every hour to the full with God's presence, and then stepping into the next hour, making every now an eternity of God's presence.

Out of this intensely "present tense" kind of living, he developed a new sense of identity, a sense of self no longer held hostage to the past. There are two of his learnings at which I have been working for all these many years; let me read them to you:

"We are what we are now, not an hour ago,
and [not] what we are planning..."

In other words, though people may judge us by our past, refusing to forgive us for what we once were; and though we may hold ourselves hostages to our past, in the eyes of a God of grace, who forgives our past and makes all things new, we are what we are now.

To this, he added another helpful word for dealing with our frequent lapses and failures in maintaining such a present-tense awareness of God's presence. He wrote this:

"... one can begin all over [again] instantly at any moment."

Just think about those two ideas together:

You are what you are right now, at this moment in time. And if what you were at any moment in the past bothers you, let it go; you are not that person any more. You are what you are now. And at every future moment in your life, whatever your failures may be, you can begin all over again instantly at any moment.

Let's work on these thoughts by asking a basic question:

ARE YOU A PRISONER OF YOUR PAST,
A HOSTAGE OF WHAT YOU HAVE BEEN?

Let's start with a little story. Back when my youngest daughter, Holly, was in high school, she was not only a very good soccer player; but also a certified referee. This gave her many opportunities to earn money as a referee in little league soccer games. Holly is very good with little children and enjoyed being with them. Most of her problems were with parents who were prone to push their children beyond their limits -- parents for whom winning was more important than the welfare of their children.

As I remember it, there was a little boy on one team who always got stuck with playing the position of goalie. He didn't like playing that position, not only because he wanted to be out on the field where the action was, but also because it was difficult for a little kid to play goalie. Whenever the other team scored a goal, he would be blamed. On one such occasion, just after the other team scored a goal, he broke down in tears and said sobbing, "I just don't want to play goalie!"

I wonder how many of us have some little childlike place within our hearts where we go to cry over the fact that we just don't want to play the part that the rest of the world has decided we must play. We're tired of being the person that the rest of the world has decided we must be. We'd like to have a life of our own, apart from the demands and expectations of the rest of the world. We'd like to be our own person and play our own part in the drama of life.

When I speak about being prisoners of our past, I'm not limiting this to a discussion of our past faults and failures. I'm talking about the cumulative and complex set of demands and expectations that the world has laid upon us through the years of our life. We all wear a heavy harness constructed by the many voices, forces, and influences that have surrounded our life up to now. There is a way in which a world of diverse influences gangs up on every life. Every one of us is forced to play goalie when we really want to play some other position.

The voices begin with our parents, who surround us with a set of certain expectations, spoken or unspoken. Of course, all of this is done -- so we parents say -- "in loving concern and for our benefit." We want our children to have all that we have had in life; indeed, we want them to have even more than what we have been able to earn and enjoy.

- I can remember a father in one of my churches who said to his sons, "You can go to any college or university that you choose, as long as it's Princeton." He wanted them to have what he had. Sometimes that works out, and sometimes it doesn't. Sometimes, going to Dad's alma mater is what we don't want, and so we fail at it. The final result is that everyone is miserable.

- I can remember another father whose life dream was that his oldest son would make it into West Point. He wanted his son to have what he could never have. And his son did gain an appointment to the academy. His father was thrilled. However, after a year, his son dropped out, shattering his father's dream. And the reason why his son became a dropout? He wanted to be like his father; he wanted to become a skillful and artistic woodworker like his dad. And he did just that, and became a smashing success, and now his father is very proud of him. Interestingly, his younger brother became a highly successful officer in the United States Navy; and his father is also glowingly proud of him. In most instances, parents end up very happy with their children, when they let their children pursue their own dreams and learn by their own mistakes along the way.

Our parents can lay all sorts of demands upon us. We must live up to the family image. We must have the proper friends. We must go to the proper school. We must make a proper marriage. We must enter the right career. Some of us comply and, having taken the course of least resistance, and having received our proper comfortable inheritance, then live (according to Thoreau) "lives of quiet desperation." Others who try to wear this harness of propriety finally break down. We snap at a moment of stress; eat, drink, or drug ourselves daily into a comfortable stupor; or break down in the relationships that have been imposed upon us.

However, it's not always our parents. Society itself is a cruel parent in telling us what we may or may not do with our lives.

- At least one half of the people born into the world have been, and still are, told that there are certain parts they may and may not play in the drama of life. All kinds of voices say "You're a woman, and we've decided what women can and can't do. It's our decision, not yours. Maybe we'll let you into the club, and maybe we won't." Much of the behavior of the adult male world toward women is like that of the gang of little kids on my block when I was a little boy. When we would build a ramshackled club house, we would post over it a sign that read "No Girls!" Such childishness still prevails, even in high places.
- Another huge segment of the human family is told at birth "Sorry, but you're black, and we'll decide what position you'll play on the team -- that is, if we decide that you can even be on the team."
- Still others are told "Sorry, you're a Jew! Go start your own club; go live in your own section of town; after all, you've got plenty of your own money." Still others are told that they're Wops, Pollocks, or Hunkies and that they have their proper place in the world of business or pleasure. My closest friend in Detroit, outside the church, was Polish; his painful experience in the business world was that his Polish name was not always an asset. And, of course, there are those who are rejected in every neighborhood because of their sexual orientation. And those of us who reject them can find all kinds of literal proof texts in a Bible that, in other instances, such as divorce and remarriage, we don't take very literally at all.

Martin Luther King was working for something much bigger than the rights of his own people; he was seeking the right of every human being to be what God made them to be. He was affirming God's creation of every human life, because it is God's creation that we reject when we tell anyone that they cannot be what and who they are. And that is, after all, the original sin: the rejection of God as the creator of our lives -- the rejection of the richness, wonder, and variety that he has willed for his entire creation. It is God's many splendored pattern for his world that we reject when we make ourselves the little lords of the world and demand that everything and everyone fit our safe sameness.

And so, we live in fear:

- fear of one another, because we have rejected God's love of variety and live at arm's length from those who might threaten the stagnant stability of our lives;
- fear for our own future, because we live with scenarios of a future in which we will never be able to escape the part and position that a sinful world has assigned to us.

How many of our sins are no more than a childish rebellion against having to play goalie? We want to be out on the field playing the game of life, contributing to the team of the human family the unique talents and gifts that are ours and ours alone. We just want a chance to be ourselves and play our own position.

Too many sermons about escaping the imprisonment of the past focus upon the sins of our past, especially our carnal sins and sexual lusts. Do you know what? I don't think God spends much time peering in bedroom windows. He knows why we have been driven to our pitiful patterns of behavior. God's concern is with the imprisonment that we have been forced to accept -- imprisonment in the demands and expectations of others. Most of our sinning is no more than a childish rebellion against having to play goalie.

Do you know who you really are?

- You are not what you have always been forced to be by others.
- You are not what you fear you will always have to be, on into a dark future that marches toward a despairing death in the desert.
- You are not what others say you are.
- You are not what you have resigned yourself into being.

You are what you are now, not even what you were an hour ago, and you can begin all over again instantly at any moment -- for that matter, right now. You can start being you!

Please don't think that I am saying that it will be easy to start all over again. It will take all the strength that you can muster to be the person God created you to be and to play the position that God equipped you to play. Indeed, for some of us, extra help is needed.

Some of us have been trapped for such a long time that we need qualified counselors and therapists to help us sort it all out. Furthermore, it won't happen overnight. The glorious truth, however, is that you can begin instantly, because there is a life-giving Spirit that can fall upon you from above to give you a new birth. You can be born all over again. There is a Holy Wind blowing through this world, which can breathe new life into the dead, dry bones of your life.

And it is never too late. Alongside Dr. Laubach's little booklet, I keep a letter that he wrote me in 1970. He was 85 years old then. We had never met, but my longtime friend, Dennis Kinlaw, President of Asbury College in Wilmore, Kentucky, had invited him to teach there. I had invited him to speak in my Louisville church. Because of the heavy schedule that he still maintained, he had to decline my invitation. His letter, which had begun with the flattering salutation "Dear Brother Roberts," ended with the benediction "God give you a tremendous fire of the Spirit."

It is never too late to light that fire. You can begin today, right now, before you leave this service of worship.

However, the first step will be painful. If you want to be released from your imprisonment, you must release all of those whom you have held hostage to their past.

- If you have ever said "That's the way he is, and I guess he'll always be that way," then say that no more. Give him a chance, in your heart and expectations, to be someone new and different. Maybe he won't change; however, whatever he does, release him!
- If you have ever said "She said that, and she did that, and I can never forget it," then relieve yourself of that bitter memory. Forget it. Give her a chance to be someone new. Maybe she won't become someone new; however, whatever she does, release her!
- If you have ever said "That's the way they are. There may be a few good ones, but the great majority will always be lazy and irresponsible," then stop saying that, because it is morally lazy and irresponsible for you to say that about any group of people. After all, look at the laziness and irresponsibility of certain spoiled grownups in your own group.

Start believing in others, hoping for the realization of their best possibilities and releasing them from the bondage of limitations in which you have held them hostage. Maybe he won't change, and maybe she'll go on saying and doing the unkind things she's always said and done, and maybe they'll go on being what they've always been. What will change is something inside yourself. You'll be free from the hatred you've always felt toward those who have held you hostage. You'll be able to lay down that burden by the riverside; you won't have to "study war no more." You'll find a new Spirit releasing you and enabling you to be your true self. You won't have to play goalie any longer; you'll be able to get out on the field and kick that ball right out of the stadium. And then, you too will be able to sing that song of freedom: "Free at last, free at last! Thank God almighty, I'm free at last!"

Traveling Toward the Promised Land*

April 24, 1994

Scripture Lesson: ***Deuteronomy 26: 1-11.***

❦

Those of you who have particularly retentive minds and can remember past sermons of mine may think that you are about to hear a warmed-over old one this morning; such is not the case. What is old is the title. It was the title of the sermon that I preached on my very last Sunday, June 2, 1985, in my church in Michigan; however, it is not that sermon. One other old feature is the opening story, which I used to get into my first sermon here in this church on the following Sunday, June 9, 1985. Because so many of you have become members of this church since then, I think it can bear retelling for the purpose of starting out today.

It's about a time back during my ministry in Birmingham when I was offered a free trip to the Holy Land. There was a fraternal organization in Detroit that made this generous offer to various clergy persons from time to time, and in this particular year, such an offer was made to me. However, even though I had never taken a Holy Land tour, it was impossible for me to do so, because I had already committed myself to be here at Pittsburgh Seminary as a Distinguished Pastor-in-Residence. So, I responded to this offer by suggesting that the tour be offered to a younger associate pastor on our staff. My suggestion was taken. The offer was made to and enjoyed by him.

Not too long after this, while I was picking up a prescription at our nearby Devon Drug Store, one of the owners of the store, my friend Norman Shapiro, began telling me, with some considerable enthusiasm, of a Holy Land tour from which he had just returned. His high excitement was all the more interesting because he had gone to Israel on several occasions. However, his previous visits were with Jewish tour groups, members of his synagogue, I presumed. This most recent tour was with a Christian tour group, and there were aspects of this tour that were new to him; he was seeing the Holy Land through a Christian perspective. Thus it was that he said, if I were ever offered such an opportunity, I should by all means go on such a tour.

When he said that, I told him that I had recently turned down an offer of a free tour to the Holy Land. Staring at me in some amazement, he asked why on earth I would ever refuse such an opportunity for cultural and spiritual enlightenment and enrichment. I responded, saying "Because I had to go to Pittsburgh." Then, in even greater astonishment, he looked at me and exclaimed, "You could have gone to the Promised Land, and you went to Pittsburgh?"

I'm glad that this celebration of my ministry is happening two weeks before my final Sunday in the pulpit, because I don't think I can get all of my farewell thoughts into that one last sermon on May 8. I also realize that what I have to share with you today is not, in the usual sense of the word, a sermon. There's a lot of personal stuff that needs to be shared -- more than one would include in a normal sermon. So, lest I disappoint those who are accustomed to my habit of almost always exploring an idea from two vantage points, let me divide my thoughts into two parts as I try to talk of some things I have learned during these 40-plus years of wandering in the wilderness.

I HAVE LEARNED THAT IT'S IMPORTANT TO BE TRAVELING TOWARD SOME KIND OF A PROMISED LAND.

The story of God's people has its real start not in the Garden of Eden, but rather in the 12th chapter of Genesis when Abraham and Sarah, the parents of all faithful people, decide to leave the great city, Ur of the Chaldees, to go chasing a dream. A much later New Testament writer, interpreting that Old Testament story, says that in doing so, Abraham "set out, not knowing where he was going." That is, Abraham's journey had no precise geographical direction;

instead, it had a spiritual orientation. Abraham was following a map inside his heart. The author of the Letter to the Hebrews says that he "looked forward to the city that has foundations, whose architect and builder is God." Call it whatever you want: the Promised Land, the Holy City, the New Jerusalem, the Impossible Dream (Don Quixote) -- whatever you call it, it's important to be drawn to and driven by something out there, something that's visible only to the eyes of the heart. Having such an invisible and impossible dream has always been important to me.

Sometime toward the end of my years in Princeton Seminary, President Mackay said something that has always stayed with me. I can't remember the occasion of his saying it, whether it was in a chapel service or a class. In some ways it was an impossible piece of advice: he said that, as we left seminary and went out to our various assignments, we should treat any and every church as a lifetime commitment. He was addressing a frequent mentality of young ministers who, as they go to their first church ("first miserable church"), think of it as a temporary stepping stone to something more important. Well, it's difficult not to think that way about one's first assignment; after all, you know you're probably not going to be there for the rest of your ministry. Still, Dr. Mackay was saying that if you feel that way, maybe you ought not to go there. He was saying, "Don't treat any church as temporary, as a stepping stone. Get unpacked. Settle down. Whatever you do, do it as though you're going to make this church your life work."

Well, that was a pretty high ideal -- and also somewhat unrealistic -- as I went to my first little church. I have often described it to you. It was only the congregation that was small; the building was much too large for that remaining remnant of what had once been a much larger congregation. It was old and in a state of disrepair beyond the resources of the faithful few who were trying to hold it together. There was even some talk about closing the church and merging with another nearby congregation. So, why think about making this a life commitment? Well, I didn't; however, what I did do was to dream.

As I have told you once before, I would dream about its being a larger congregation, and when I preached, I would write the best sermons I could, as though they were being written for a great congregation. And having done that, when the time came to enter the pulpit, I would "psych" myself up by pretending that I was preaching to a full house. Henry Ward Beecher had once preached to a full house in that sanctuary in bygone days. And so now, every Sunday, I would pretend that the dusty, empty gallery was full and I would preach as though addressing that imaginary full house. I guess I threw myself into it so heartily that, on one Sunday, one old-timer looked back up into the balcony to see who might be sitting up there.

Well, maybe that's not the best way for a young preacher to deal with such a declining church situation; however, my re-imagining at least inspired me to preach the best sermons I could. That method of preaching to a make-believe congregation had the quixotic result of helping me to treat the handful of old folks who gathered every Sunday as though they were a great congregation. What I had to say was surely not very great, but it was the very best I could do at that point in my development as a preacher.

Not too many years later, we moved out of that old building in downtown Newburgh and into a Hudson River Tudor mansion, where we turned a ballroom into a sanctuary. It was a lovely estate surrounded by a stone wall, with beautiful trees, gardens, and plantings. What a fairyland it was for raising our little Hillie, who was only a year old when we moved in. In later years, she would write a high school composition about it entitled "When I Was a Princess."

In some ways, moving into that estate was the fulfillment of the dream, and I actually began to think at times that I might spend my entire ministry there. At least, moving there was moving closer to the dream. Still, what is interesting is the way in which the dream of some majestic sanctuary reverberating with the anthems of a great choir would not go away. It's not that I was dissatisfied with where I was or what I was doing; for that matter, I loved those years at Union Church. It was just that there was always something out there beckoning to me. I remember how I would listen to a recording of great anthems by the Robert Shaw Chorale, and how, as I listened, I felt that some church in a land of far-off dreams was calling to me.

The good thing about that mysterious longing was that, instead of making me unhappy with where I was, it helped me all the more to treat my present church as a great church and to continue striving for excellence in the pulpit.

Well, the years went by, and I moved on to other churches in Mount Vernon, Louisville, Birmingham, and finally here to Shadyside. And in some sense, every move seemed to carry me closer to the dream. Each church had its strengths and weaknesses, its problems and challenges; each was unique in some way and in each, the music seemed to get better and better. Whenever it came time to leave, parting was always very difficult and tearful for me; however, I was always thrilled by the challenge of the next church to which I was going, and I always enjoyed the good providence of being able to go to some ministry that was interestingly different from the one before.

I think I can honestly say that there was a thrill to every call, and that each church seemed like some kind of dream coming true. Each church was somehow a fulfillment of that invisible dream, which was gradually working itself out. And each church, therefore, became a challenge to work all the harder at my preaching. So, maybe I can say that each church, in its own way, was a dream church (even though each had its own nightmares). Whatever the problems week after week, in my imagination I saw each church as a congregation that deserved the best I could do. And nothing was so agonizing as those Sundays when, for some reason, the sermon was not all that I wanted it to be. In that sense, I have been a driven man -- driven, however, by the belief that out there in front of me was some kind of great congregation waiting for some good word from God.

I believe that there are dreams that are energizing, and that God has some dream plan that he is trying to fulfill in every life. I don't know what God's dream is for you, but I believe that he has one and that it is important for you to keep seeking that dream. Make sure that it is somewhat impossible, and don't ever confuse a dream with some easily attainable goal. Make sure it's a big enough dream, and remember that it may take you most of your life to get to the Promised Land. But even if you spend all your life getting there and have only a few years left to enjoy it, it will still be worth it because you won't be you until you get there.

Just remember something: when you fall asleep at night (or else when you wake up in the middle of the night) wondering what your life is about, when you're going to see light at the end of the tunnel, when your dream will come true -- just remember that God lies awake with you, and that your life is his dream, and that he wants you to be everything he created you to be.

You may be different from others, and your dream may not be their dream; but don't ever forget that you yourself are God's dream, that he has planted his dream in your heart, and that he wants it to come true more than you ever could. So dream on, because it is God who is dreaming his dream in your life and leading you, step by step, to your Camelot. Paul put it this way: "Work out your own salvation with fear and trembling, for it is God who is at work in you, enabling you both to will and to work for his good pleasure."

And when you get to the Promised Land, you'll understand a second truth, and it is this:

AS YOU HAVE BEEN TRAVELING TOWARD THE PROMISED LAND, YOU HAVE REALLY BEEN THERE ALL ALONG.

As I look back over these 41 years of ministry, there's not a place along the way that was not, in some sense, a piece of the Promised Land. That doesn't mean that I made no mistakes; I made many. Nor does it mean that I might not have done it some other way; there are all kinds of ways in which God can work out his plan in our lives. What I am saying is that at some point along the way I realized that God has his purpose in every step of the journey.

Every person is sent into your life for some good purpose, and we must affirm each one of them. So I can say that I have been blessed with both wonderful friends and enemies. I cannot begin to tell you how many wonderful friends I have had.

There was a time in my first church when a much larger church wanted to call me as Associate Pastor. Because it was not far away, I had to write my own church members to tell them about my intention to accept such a call. When the members of my little church received my letter, they did something unconstitutional. They held their own unofficial congregational meeting in the sanctuary. After they had discussed the matter, they called me into the meeting and told me all the reasons why I shouldn't accept the call. They wanted to offer me a salary increase, which I would not accept; however, I did consent to stay and turned down the call to the other church. The next day, one of the fine older women of that church, Charlotte Tyler, talked to me in the church kitchen about the meeting. I have never forgotten what she said. She put her hands on my shoulders, as though talking to her son, and said, "Now Morgan, we know that you'll be leaving here some day; but this was not what we wanted for you!" In other words, this church thought of me as their son. They had taken me as a boy preacher out of seminary and were training me for my future ministry. And this was not in their plan. Really, now, can you imagine being loved that much by a church, and do you realize how much it does for one's growth and development in ministry to be so loved.

And I've had some grand enemies, too; and I needed every one of them. Some of them, given enough time, became my good friends. And others remained always opponents. However, there was always one factor that kept me from hating them. I realized that if they had ever known how really bad I was, they would have opposed me even more. Still, their opposition kept me alert and on my knees, and made me think carefully and charitably through our points of difference. That's one of the great values of having enemies; they help you to think clearly and demand that you deal fairly. So, I thank God for all of them!

Let me say also that every experience is sent into your life for some purpose, and that there is something to be learned from all the good and bad experiences, especially those involving failure.

Sometimes I try to speculate on how different my life might have been had I not made some of the really bad mistakes that I have made. I think of other directions that I might have taken, and of other roads that I might have traveled.

Then too, I think of the years that are wasted when we travel on the wrong road. But, whenever you start trying to rethink predestination, you realize that, had you taken some other road, some of the best things in your life could not have taken place. Just think, on some other road, our four adopted children might not have come our way. Some very good things in life can only happen on the wrong road. So, give thanks for every step of the journey on any and every road. Affirm all your failures, mistakes, and bad decisions -- all of them were important.

For that matter, don't spend a lot of time looking back on the roadways of the past, whether marked by success or failure. Learn to let go of everything in the past; if you don't do that, you will really get old and die. The journey never ends, and as long as you keep chasing your dream, you'll enjoy all the new persons and experiences that God places in your pathway. You will know that you are already in the promised land and that, as Thoreau said, "Heaven is under our feet as well as over our heads."

To bring all of this to a conclusion, let me quote from a magnet affixed to our refrigerator up in the country. It reads "Whenever you see a turtle on top of a fence post, you know he's had lots of help." And maybe that's the best way to tell about my journey as I near the end of one road, before setting out on another. The dream that I have followed is not mine; it is God's dream. I could never have dreamed up anything so wonderfully fulfilling and surprising as the unfolding dream of my life. And I have not walked alone as I have followed that dream. I have had lots of encouragement and support, along with tons of patience and forgiveness. I thank God for all of you, friends and foes, who have walked the road with me.

Let me bring this sermon to a close with a prayer of Thomas Merton, which I have carried with me for many years:

My Lord God, I have no idea where I am going. I do not see the road ahead of me. I cannot know for certain where it will end. Nor do I really know myself, and the fact that I think I am following your will does not mean that I am actually doing so. But I believe that the desire to please you does in fact please you. And I hope that I will never do anything apart from that desire. And I know that if I do this, you will lead me by the right road, though I may know nothing about it. Therefore, I will trust you always, though I may seem to be lost and in the shadow of death. I will not fear, for you are ever with me, and you will never leave me to face my perils alone.

Thomas Merton, Thoughts in Solitude

* This sermon was preached on the Sunday of Dr. Roberts' retirement.

$\mathcal{C}$hurch Full of Winners

May 1, 1994

Scripture Lesson: **Galatians 3: 23-29; I Peter 2: 13 - 3: 7.**

$\mathscr{I}$ have never preached a sermon that has mentioned much, if anything at all, about the Pittsburgh Marathon, which has since its inception been run on this first Sunday in May. One of the reasons for my silence has been the disregard demonstrated by previous city administrations for the concerns of city churches about this event. Because some of our city churches are adversely affected by the severe restrictions that the race course imposes upon the movement of traffic to and from our churches, there have been meetings with city officials to discuss these problems. Back in the beginning, when I attended such meetings, even though we proposed alternatives that would have been beneficial and probably even profitable to all concerned parties (particularly to retail merchants), the treatment that we received was that of polite disregard. I am led to believe, however, that the new city administration is moving in a much more positive direction.

Although it no longer matters what I think (being a "lame duck" who is now leaving the city), I have made this opening comment so that I can qualify it with a contrasting comment of a positive nature. My comment is this: I think the Marathon is one of the greatest sporting events in the city of Pittsburgh. For me, its only equal is the "Great Race," which I think is the greatest sporting event in Pittsburgh. Now I realize that there are several other sports that claim a rather large amount of attention in Pittsburgh. If I recall correctly, we have a baseball team, a hockey team, and a football team. Still, despite the huge amount of attention that these sports receive, plus the benefits that accrue to the city because of them -- and also in respect to my dear departed father who played professional baseball on some long ago farm team -- still, I say that the Marathon and the Great Race are the greatest sporting events in Pittsburgh. I also say that their counterparts in other cities of the world are the greatest sporting events in those cities. Why do I say this?

I say it because running, like no other sport, has an inherent capability of attracting an incalculable number of people into healthy, vigorous exercise and participation. I can think of no other sport that requires so minimal an investment in time and equipment; that can be enjoyed anytime and anywhere by almost anyone; that can be done alone or with others; and that, as a competitive sporting event, invites all comers.

There is no sporting activity that can match running in its democracy and availability. You can pack your running shoes and togs into your suitcase wherever you go. It is one of the easiest ways to sightsee in a strange city. Despite a few horror stories, runners hardly ever get mugged; they don't carry wallets. When you're running, you can enjoy the sights slowly, without worrying about one-way streets or traffic jams. I have run across the Golden Gate Bridge in San Francisco, enjoying the morning fog at a slow pace. That is impossible if you're driving. I ran around the capital buildings in Harrisburg on a crisp, cold autumn evening, hopping up their stairways in boyish pleasure. I ran along the ocean at Pebble Beach, enjoying the view at a substantially lower cost than those who were playing golf. I have crossed the upper reaches of the Mississippi in Minneapolis and have run across the bridge from Kentucky to Indiana, just so I could say that I ran in two states in the same day. And whenever and wherever I have done these things, I have enjoyed a friendly runners' wave from other runners, old and young, male and female, rich or poor, who were enjoying the same utterly available and democratic activity.

Of course, there was a time, not too long ago, when running did not enjoy such broad and universal participation by so many people of so many ages and social stations in life.

I can remember running in road races in the 1940's in which, perhaps, as few as a dozen contestants lined up on the starting line --

so few that each runner was introduced by name to the crowd, somewhat like a TV announcer names race horses as they are pushed into the starting gate. There were some large races, like the National Inter-Scholastics held in Van Cortlandt Park in New York City, which drew 500 runners; however, even local small-town road races nowadays will draw twice or three times that number. Back then, you couldn't see what you see nowadays: all kinds of people at all hours of the day out on the streets having their daily run. Running was the sport of those few "crazies" who enjoyed the pain of running long distances with few, if any, spectators cheering them on along the way or applauding them at the finish line.

Maybe the best way to illustrate the amazing inclusivity of running is with a story about a marathon which I watched go by. This goes back to about 1981 or so. We had been on summer vacation up in Canada near a ski resort about an hour from Montreal. We were returning home at mid-morning when traffic suddenly came to a halt on the outskirts of Montreal. The last runners in the Montreal marathon were passing by. It was a delay we had not anticipated; however, it was not one that I resented. At the time, I was running 50 miles every week, hoping to run in the Detroit marathon (a hope that didn't happen). Anyway, the last stragglers passed by, and traffic began moving again. And then, about five miles down the road, we saw him. We came upon the runner who was running dead last in that marathon. He was moving very deliberately and rather painfully. If ever there was a depiction of the so-called "loneliness of the long distance runner," he was it. But he was lonely in an added sense; he had only one leg and was running with crutches.

In my life, I have been to a few great sporting events, including seven Kentucky Derbies. But for me, watching that lonely disabled man running on crutches was the greatest moment in sports that I think I will ever experience. Someone, far, far ahead of him was declared the winner that day. Then, too, as in all running events, there were those who won the various age and gender divisions (another democratizing feature of running); however, when that special man crossed the finish line many hours later on that day, surely he had to be a winner who had more "class" than any other winner in that race.

You see why, for what are almost spiritual reasons, I call this the greatest sporting event. In a road race, no one is a loser. As the participants in today's marathon cross the finish line down at Point State Park, there will be many miles between the first and the last. Some will be running, some will be walking, some will be in wheelchairs. Some will be young and lean; others will be older and a little lumpy. However, as each one crosses the finish line, no one in the crowd will shout "loser." No one will suggest that those in the back of the pack don't belong in the race. Indeed, it wouldn't be much of a race without them. How much of a crowd would turn out to watch 20 runners compete? The genius of running is that anyone can be in the race, and everyone, even those who have to drop out because of injury or fatigue -- everyone in the race is a winner. This is a race full of winners. What a pity that the Presbyterian Church can't learn a lesson from that race! How sad that our denomination can't catch the spirit of the marathon!

I chose this morning's lessons for the purpose of illustrating the incredible diversity and inclusivity of the New Testament church. Of course, when we talk about the so-called New Testament church, we are talking about a many-splendored creature, which spanned three generations and had grown sporadically and spontaneously. It came to include a spectrum of belief and practice as wide as anything that we have in the great variety of churches that exist today.

Indeed, at the time when the New Testament documents were put together in a final canonical collection of official scriptures, there was more diversity than we have in the church today. Some examples:

• In the early churches in Galatia to which Paul wrote, the idea of equality between male and female, Jew and Gentile, slaves and masters was at least being talked about.

• On the other hand, in most other churches women were assigned to a terribly subordinate place, far, far below the place that they hold in today's churches. Slavery was not only accepted, but condoned and approved as an institution to be respected and observed. After all, Paul sent a runaway slave back to his master.

- Some Christians believed that Jesus would be returning in their own lifetime; others placed that final event in a somewhat delayed future.
- Some Christians practiced orderly forms of worship, while in other churches people babbled in tongues as in today's Pentecostal churches.
- Some Christians came to have the beginnings of a hierarchical structure, while the Johannine churches believed in no structure other than the leading of the Holy Spirit.

What is amazing is that in the fourth century, when the New Testament was being put together and when the thrust was toward uniformity, those who made the decisions about what would be Christian scripture did not edit this diversity out of the New Testament. They let it stand with its impossible diversity of belief and practice. Somehow or other, anyone who loved Jesus was welcomed into the race!

And you know, it's not quite that way today in the Presbyterian Church. Granted, we have made some substantial progress. We have come a long way from the day when what was defined as the "great churches" of our denomination were those few that were large and wealthy, led by great male preachers and governed by the important men in the community. From such a male-dominated church, we have made strides toward being a church in which women and minorities are, at last, allowed to be in the race.

Still, granting all of that progress, the race that is run in the life of the church is a handicap race in which women and minorities must run under a heavier handicap. When a church seeks to fill a vacant pulpit, a woman preacher has to be far more than equal to compete with the male preachers. There is only one church in our entire denomination with a membership exceeding 1,500 members in which a woman serves as preaching pastor (and she will be preaching here in Shadyside Church in the coming year). Surely, there cannot be such a shortage of capable women pastors as to account for this strange absence of women in major pulpits. Approximately one-third of the students in our seminaries are women, many of whom have had successful careers in business, industry, and the professions. Surely, there must have been more than one graduate over the past 20 years who is capable of leading a large congregation. The reality, however, is that highly skilled women find difficulty in getting called to even the medium-sized churches.

What is provocative about the response to the Re-Imagining Conference is that it has focused fiercely upon a controversial theological issue and not upon a whole host of other conference subjects. Those subjects reflect the frustration of women in their desire to be full participants in a church in which they are and always have been in the majority. Indeed, the attack upon participants in that conference has been vicious and distorted, and the Presbyterian Layman organization has used it as a means for dividing and destroying the Presbyterian Church.

There should be full debate of any and all theological issues raised by that conference, especially because of the pressing need to reach theological expressions that are solidly Biblical, but also inclusive and affirming of women in the church. However, the attempt to strangle such debate by suggesting that churches withhold even their share of the operating expenses of our denomination is unconscionable, divisive, and dishonoring to the cause of Jesus Christ. There must be room for the entire range of theological expression in our denomination -- room for conservative evangelicals as well as for those of other alternative positions. However, what the church cannot tolerate is the attitude that demands that there be only one possible expression of orthodoxy and that those who do not submit to that one definition may not be in the race. If women are not free to gather and explore ways to become full participants in a system that is not open and working for them, the church surely is in peril.

And along with that, of course, is the matter of another silent minority within every church: our gay and lesbian members. They are not waiting to get into our churches; they are and always have been there. They have served in every possible role in our churches. They have taught our Sunday School children, sung in our choirs, served on our boards, supported us with sacrificial giving, filled our pulpits -- but at a very high price to their inherent personhood: the price of remaining silent about their identity. Still, they have remained in our churches at the price of pretending that they are someone other than they actually are, the price of leading a double life, or else the price of living without a committed relationship of intimacy, which is the right of every human being.

And now, our denomination has singled them out for special second-class citizenship: they may be members of our church; however, they may not serve as ordained officers. Theirs is now a special class of limited membership. They may sit on the sidelines while the normal members run the race. No such class of membership exists for divorced or greedy persons (and the New Testament has far more to say about divorce and greed than about homosexuality). In our interpretation of the New Testament, we are very selective. There are things that we have come to overlook. There are matters, like slavery, about which we would say that we now know that the New Testament writers were wrong. When will we be willing to admit that the New Testament writers were wrong when they described homosexuality as voluntary? When will we be able to say that homosexuality is neither a sin nor a disease; it just is. Just as we have different color skin, hair, and eyes, we also have different sexual orientations. Is it that we don't know this, or is it that there is something in us that needs to keep certain people out of the race?

You know, in all of the turmoil that boils within our denomination today, there may be a magnificent opportunity: the chance to become again something like the New Testament church in which people with impossible differences somehow stayed together. I don't want a church that has been deserted by the evangelicals. I don't even want them to change their minds about their most cherished beliefs. My beginnings were in that camp, and that's why, every so often, we sing an old gospel hymn. So, I want them to stay in the Presbyterian Church, but not if they demand that we all agree with them. I envision a church in which people who will never agree will continue to talk and debate and pray together, but with one basic provision: we will never question the sincerity of one another's faith, and we will never tell anyone that they can't be in the race and run it in their own way and at their own speed. We can become a church full of winners!

The race of faith is not like a road race. In the race set before us with Jesus, we don't know who's leading the pack. We might be surprised to find out that some rather undesirable or different souls are running closer to him than we could ever realize. In the race of faith, as in a marathon, you have to run it by yourself; no one can run it for you. And if you run it well, you won't have time to watch others.

I found it moving to see Mike Bonn sitting with those special guests whom I asked to have invited to my farewell bash. Some of you newcomers may not know that it was Mike Bonn who led the first Easter demonstration against our church in 1984. What is difficult for us to understand is that he did that because he felt it to be his Christian duty. I don't know how he feels about what he did back then; I don't know how his mind has changed. What matters is that people who run with Christ in different ways can live together. For that matter, if we can't, what hope is there for the world! After all, when we attack one another viciously and withdraw support from the mission and ministry of the church, what kind of signal does that send to the world.

When I left my church in Michigan, they had a farewell thing for me there, too. One of those who spoke was the pastor of the inner city church where I worked in the soup kitchen every Friday morning. At the conclusion of his remarks, he presented me with a towel in the hope that, in coming here, I would never forget the servant Lord who took a towel and washed the disciples' feet.

There have been lots of eras of theological debate in the history of the church; they never hurt the church. However, the vital times in the ministry and mission of the church have not been those when we fought over theology, but rather those times when we fought over the towel to see how we could outdo one another in humble, lowly service. This is no time to throw in the towel. We need to listen to one another and serve one another, and we cannot do this if we go sulking off into our little corners. Indeed, this is a time when we must be running together, running with patience the race which is set before us, "looking to Jesus the pioneer and perfecter of our faith, who for the sake of the joy that was set before him, endured the cross, disregarding its shame, and has taken his seat at the right hand of the throne of God." Now there's a winner!

❦

ℋ House of New Beginnings

May 8, 1994

*Scripture Lesson: **John 14 (Selections)**.*

here comes to be a great deal of interest and expectation surrounding one's last sermon in any church, and if it is the last sermon of one's so-called active ministry, the level of attention is even higher. I remember how much I expected when Garrison Keillor was to deliver what was to be his last "News From Lake Wobegon" on the old and original *Prairie Home Companion*. And I remember how much I felt let down when it didn't measure up to his usual standard. So, I hope that I will not disappoint you in what are some final thoughts as I take leave of Shadyside Church, before embarking on a try at some interim pastorate ministries.

This parting moment is heightened by the lovely surprises that have been showered upon me during these last weeks; I have alluded to them in writing in today's bulletin. There have been moments when I have actually felt exhausted by so much kindness, and now you have added to all of this, by graciously designating me your Pastor Emeritus. So, where shall I begin?

Over the years, I have learned much from the style of E. B. White, and there is a word of his that expresses some of my feelings as I begin today. Concerning the successes of his writing career about which he felt shy and uncomfortable, he once said that he often felt like a clown of average ability whose signals got crossed and who found himself out on the high wire with the Flying Wallendas. I have often felt that way as I have been called to larger and larger responsibilities, from one church to the next. Some voice within me has whispered the question "What are you doing here?" How does a kid from a blue-collar neighborhood whose father had only a fifth-grade education and whose mother gave up school to go to work after ninth grade -- how does such a boy arrive finally in such fine churches as those it has been my privilege to serve?

Well, I don't have the answer to those questions, but White's metaphor has a secondary meaning for me because of a conviction I hold: there is a clown role to which every faithful preacher is called. I am obviously not referring to those tiresome ministers who always have some weekly funny story to begin a sermon, although humor is a wonderful pulpit tool when used adroitly. Instead, I refer to the clown role of the minister as a prophetic humorist -- someone who is called to puncture the swollen balloon of pomposity that surrounds much of human life. A good preacher will often quietly laugh at him or herself before the congregation in the hope of helping others to learn that same healthy laughter that relieves us of self-seriousness. Another good writer and humorist, Robert Traver (who wrote *Anatomy of a Murder*), spoke in this spirit when referring to his love of fishing. He said he loved to fish "not because I regard fishing as being so terribly important, but because I suspect that so many of the other concerns of men are equally unimportant -- and not nearly so much fun."

A preacher should be a good clown in helping people to laugh at the manner in which so many really unimportant things in life suffocate us in self-seriousness. Not until we learn how much of our life is unimportant can we ever know what it is that really matters.

I think a case can be made for the assertion that, in the words and deeds of Jesus, we can often detect the function of the prophetic clown. A New York World's Fair film in 1964 depicted Jesus in the role of a clown. It elicited something of a storm of criticism, notably from a host of very serious and somber preachers whose fury probably proved the point. That was the very reaction Jesus produced in the overly serious religious leaders of his day. They couldn't stand him. He wouldn't take their seriousness seriously. People make such a production of life (particularly religious people), and in the complications caused by their compulsion to be some-body, they miss so much of the simple music and laughter of life -- so much of the heart's ease and merriment with which life can be lived.

I have not come upon too many sermons (if any) that have talked about the merriment of Jesus. He has been painted in such dark shades that it is almost impossible for us to read the New Testament and discover this facet of his personality. However, G. K. Chesterton did detect this vein of silver laughter in the person of Jesus, and of it he wrote this:

"I say it with reverence: there was in that shattering personality a thread that must be called shyness. There was something that He hid from all men when He went up a mountain to pray. There was something that He covered constantly by abrupt silence or impetuous isolation. There was some one thing that was too great for God to show us when He walked upon our earth: And I have sometimes fancied that it was his mirth."

So what was the source of this secret stream of quiet joy that flowed as a deep current through the "thick and thin" of Jesus' life experience? Whence that holy mirth that pervaded the life of Jesus? As I attempt to answer this, I will be sharing with you the one conviction that I hold about Jesus of Nazareth. For me, it makes true joy possible in a world like ours. And it is this: the source of his mirth was Jesus' realization that he could be "at home" in our life -- that in one sense, Jesus had "come to stay."

- Because he was one with God the Father, Jesus' life in the world did not represent a life of separation from his heavenly Father. He never left his Father's eternal presence.
- He knew that there could be a home for him in the hearts of his people and that, following his death, by the indwelling presence of the Holy Spirit, he would enter into a spiritual incarnation. He would find a home in the lives of those who loved him.

This is the understanding of Jesus that we derive from the Gospel of John. Although we can arrive at other understandings of Jesus from other New Testament writings, in the fourth gospel Jesus lives with a sense of eternal joy in the here and now. In the Gospel of John, there is a distinctive emphasis upon an already realized future. Some New Testament Christians looked backwards to the days of the apostles, emphasizing the importance of keeping the faith, holding onto the past. Still other New Testament Christians looked forward to the future return of Jesus, but Johannine Christians believed that Jesus had never really gone away, that he had come to stay, and that Jesus and his Father were at home in their present day church and in their present day lives. Thus, the Johannine Jesus lives with a deep sense of mirth, and with this same sense of mirth we can live our lives. Our realization of this "eternal now" has deeply personal implications.

I often wish that we had kept a diary as we raised our twin sons, David and Dwight. Though it was a joy to raise all four of our adopted children, it was a joyful curiosity to raise twin sons. From time to time their antics and adventures have provided me with ample and apt preaching material.

Those of you who have raised any child know or remember that there comes a time when it becomes difficult to keep them in a crib. While you as a parent still need the feelings of security that come from knowing that they are penned in for the night, they begin to find ways to climb out of the crib. This is somewhat dangerous and causes you a reverse anxiety. During this stage, it is a no-win situation for you; you want the security of having them in their cribs, but you're also concerned about their climbing out.

Of course, when this situation arises with twins, they have an added inducement to climb out of their cribs: they want to be together, engaging in all kinds of night-time adventures. Thus it was that, during this stage, having escaped from their cribs in the dark, we would later find them curled up together on the floor, having finally fallen asleep. Sometimes they would be under one of the cribs, having pretended that it was a fort or clubhouse. Most times, they would collapse in sleep in front of the window, having spent their final moments before sleep watching for the possible emergence of the fire engine from the nearby fire station. Obviously, the time had come for twin beds.

We made much of the purchase of those twin beds, reminding them that they were no longer babies, but big boys who were going to be sleeping separately in big beds. Right? Wrong! To make this transition easier, when we set the new beds up, we pushed them next to one another so that they would not be far apart. We emphasized how, with this new arrangement, they could enjoy their separateness, without being far apart. No more rambling about in the dark. Every night, we would remind them of this new arrangement. Every night, they would agree to it and express satisfaction at having their own beds. And every night, when we went in for a final check, they would be entwined together in one bed. In the morning, they had no memory of having done so. It was as though there was some involuntary magnetic force that brought them together in the dark. Some mystical sense of union, some secret bond made them inseparable. They were irresistibly drawn to one another.

Do you know that God is irresistibly drawn to you? God is not up in some high heaven, watching you from a distance like a pietistic snoop, spying on your night-time activities. (The God whom some preachers proclaim often looks like a moralistic voyeur -- a God obsessed with sex, who can't wait to pounce upon the failures of his creatures.) But the God whom Jesus came to incarnate is so identified with you, so identical to you, that he cannot stay away and apart from you. In the darkest night of your soul, he is there beside you, helplessly, irresistibly entangled and entwined with your soul.

You see, God not only loves us -- God likes us! God sees some part of the divine image and likeness in every life. The reasons are these: (1) we bear God's likeness, and (2) God has taken upon himself our likeness. Consider this:

1) We are identified with God by creation. God made us the way we are, and the way we are is okay with God. This is what the doctrine of creation is really about. At the end of every day (and creation is still going on), God sits back and says that it is "very good." That's what God said on the day you were born. God saw all the work that he had done on you and proclaimed it to be very good. And that goes for women as well as men! Remember what the creation story says (Gen. 1: 27): "So God created humankind in his image, in the image of God he created them; male and female he created them." There it is in print: there is femininity in God's own nature; we all bear God's image by creation!

2) However, it gets even better. We bear God's image by redemption. To reinforce his delight in us as his creations, when we

had run away from home, God came down to earth and took upon our image and likeness! God's divine nature entered into a human nature. The Word became flesh; God actually became "bone of our bones and flesh of our flesh."

How can we doubt that God both loves us and likes us? We are identified with God both by creation and redemption. Is it any wonder that he wants to make his home in our hearts? In Jesus Christ, God has provided all that we need for mirthful living. There is nothing that you can or need to do to make yourself more lovable and likable to God. You can stop making a production of life -- stop taking your human attainments so seriously. You need only make a humble home for the Lord Jesus in your heart. Your heart is the only home that he desires. You're just fine the way you are!

There will be times when you won't sense God's presence. Indeed, there will be times when you'll think he has given up on you, because you've tried to run away from him. There will be times when you've said what you never thought you would say and done what you never thought you would do -- times of utter failure. And there will be times of utter disaster, when people do things to you that are unimaginably cruel and hateful, or when some natural, physical, or emotional disaster wipes you away. However, in those dark nights, don't forget Paul's promise that nothing "will be able to separate us from the love of God in Christ Jesus our Lord." However dark and lonely it may seem, Jesus himself will be drawn to your side. He will be entwined with you in whatever happens, because he has made his home in your heart.

And so I repeat to you again as parting words both Chesterton's statement and the wonderful promise of Jesus:

"There was some one thing that was too great for God to show us when He walked upon our earth: And I have sometimes fancied that it was his mirth."

Live your life in the mirth of our savior, remembering his words: "In the world ye shall have tribulation: but be of good cheer; I have overcome the world."

❦